MURDERS

THAT MADE HEADLINES

Cutler Funeral Home in La Porte, Indiana, is still in business more than a century after the Belle Gunness murders. The remains of women and children who would be buried locally were carried in hearses pulled by white horses; black horses pulled the bodies of men, many of whom had expected to marry a beautiful widow and found Belle instead. Photo courtesy of the La Porte County Historical Society.

JANE SIMON AMMESON

MURDERS
THAT MADE HEADLINES

CRIMES OF INDIANA

INDIANA UNIVERSITY PRESS

This book is a publication of

Indiana University Press
Office of Scholarly Publishing
Herman B Wells Library 350
1320 East 10th Street
Bloomington, Indiana 47405 USA

iupress.indiana.edu

Manufactured in the United States of America

Cataloging information is available from the Library of Congress.

ISBN 978-0-253-03126-6 (cloth)
ISBN 978-0-253-02983-6 (paperback)
ISBN 978-0-253-03127-3 (ebook)

1   2   3   4   5   22   21   20   19   18   17

CONTENTS

INTRODUCTION

WHEN PEOPLE ASKED what I was working on and I told of days reading newspaper accounts, culling death certificates and trial transcripts of old murders, and learning about such products as the wonderfully named Rough on Rats, they reacted in two distinct ways. Some were rather appalled that I revel in news articles about midnight exhumations, beheadings, and running a burial service for murderers who need a place to hide their bodies (a true niche business). Others were just as fascinated as me.

The settings for the murders I included in this book take us from the late 1850s to the Jazz Age; from travel by horse and buggy and riverboats to Hudson sedans and Cadillacs; from women wearing long dresses to flappers in short skirts; from gas lamps to electricity. But the passions that led to murder are similar to what we read and hear about today: unwanted babies, financial gain, or an impediment to marrying. Indiana was also the locale for one of the largest mass murders in the country, committed by a woman no less. Juries were just as whimsical and unpredictable then as we think of them today.

But there were differences too.

Lynching was still abided; authorities often looked the other way and perpetrators were not punished. Although I had known that the lynching of African Americans continued long into the twentieth century in the South, I was amazed that lynching occurred with regularity in Indiana, mainly Southern Indiana, until the early 1900s. There was even a double lynching as late as 1930 in Marion. It wasn't just blacks who were given that swift injustice. More whites than blacks were lynched in Indiana by about three to one and it was often sanctioned by authorities. Even some of the reporters of smaller town newspapers at the time watched on the lynchings, along with crowds of townspeople. Some took a jocular tone toward the lawlessness of the practice in their reporting.

Indiana had a governor who rescinded previous antilynching laws and was himself one of the notorious White Caps, a group of men who broke into jails to bring justice to those they thought deserved it or maybe just those they didn't like. Townspeople seemed to enjoy these little midnight soirees and descended on the bonfires or hanging trees to watch, one assumes, with pleasure while someone they knew killed another person they knew. Often, if justice had been allowed to take its course, they would have learned the person was innocent. But their philosophy was "why wait."

Before the laws changed allowing medical students access to cadavers, there was a very lucrative underground (excuse my pun) business for resurrectionists—men who didn't mind the dirty work of digging up bodies to sell. When the police decided to crack down on body snatching back in the late 1800s, medical schools, needing to dispose of their illegal cadavers, started dumping them on the streets—not the sight you'd easily imagine today in glittery and trendy downtown Indianapolis, a place filled with great restaurants, sports complexes, stores, hotels, and condos.

For Carrie Selvage, whose body disappeared in Indianapolis in 1900, the crime was at first blamed on one of the many rival groups of remnant men. Body snatchers didn't care whether their catch was rich, poor, young, or old, it just had to be fresh. One of the men was the father of future president William Henry Harrison, at the time an up and coming Indianapolis attorney, and the other his cousin. Both were found intact in medical schools. The Masons exhumed (without a permit as far as I can determine) a fellow Mason who they thought had been poisoned by his wife. His stomach was removed and shipped in a jar by boat to Louisville. And yes, they found strychnine. Charles Koesters's two children, wife, and parents were all dug up, though by medical experts in this case, to see if they had been poisoned—they had. One fascinating fact—the autopsy of Charles's mother was done in an upstairs bedroom of her home.

Which leads me to something else I learned while writing this book—record keeping. Marriage records in Indiana date back to 1788 when they were required for those residing in the Northwest Territories. The recording of births wasn't mandatory until 1882. Recording deaths began in a few Indiana cities as early as the 1870s, but the first law requiring county registration of death was passed in 1882. It wasn't until 1900 that all deaths were to be registered with the state. Compliance with the law varied until 1920 when deaths that occurred were always recorded. Imagine that. Tired of Harry after meeting the new horse and buggy doctor in town? Slip him a little arsenic and get him in the ground as fast as you can.

Poisoning, I also learned, must be addictive because poisoners seem never to have stopped at one (though that's maybe why they got caught).

People often pine for the good old days when life was simple, but believe me it wasn't.

Minnie Mabbitt went to trial along with her two brothers for the killing of her young babe. Years earlier one of the brothers and her father helped lynch her sister's lover. Now there's a Jerry Springer show for you.

As everyone who dives deep into data in a time where records were written in the old-fashioned Palmer style with big and little loops knows, documents can be difficult to decipher and names seem to mysteriously change as does other pertinent information. Take Catharine Reiff, the Hoosier Lucretia Borgia. Her maiden name is spelled in various ways such as Shoemaker and Schumacher, her first name always with an "a" where most of us would put an "e." But when I found her tombstone (thank you, Find-A-Grave), her name was etched on the stone as Rachel Katherine Schumaker. Rachel? I had never seen that name on any of the numerous legal documents bearing her name—and believe me there were a lot.

Do you know how many variations there are of the name Herskovitz? Nettie D. Sachs Zauderer Herskovitz Golden Diamond's husband, Dr. Samuel Herskovitz, spelled his name one way, and his brother, an attorney who lived in the same town, spelled his as Hershcovitz. Then there's Herscovitz, Hershcowitz, Herskovitz, Hershkovitz, and on and on. I discovered Nettie's first husband (or was it second, we're still not sure) when a genealogist at the Allen County Public Library took Zander, the only spelling I had at the time, and let Soundex spit out other alternatives. Suddenly I had Zauder then Zauderer and bingo! But to make matters more confusing, Zanderer is the way it is spelled in her divorce proceedings. Sigh.

Ages vary as well. Nettie has one age listed on her tombstone (thirty-seven), another on her death certificate (thirty-three), and on census forms, she manages to remain twenty-nine for several years. Additionally, Louis Zauderer told the newspapers Nettie was fifteen when they married in 1902, which is also the year she started pharmacy school. Yet the newspapers of the time have her age as forty-two and though I've never been able to find the original source, anecdotal information supports that number. But for a woman who can lie on a death certificate—all I can say is, Wow!

There are people you meet again and again in old newspapers. I feel as though Indianapolis coroner Manker and I are friends now since he is involved in a couple of my murder stories. At times I'd be following a case, fascinated by the storyline, and then suddenly it would be gone as though someone turned off the TV in the middle of a show. The story of Jane (or Hannah) Dorsey is one such story. She is said to have murdered four husbands, two stepchildren, her mother and sister, so my friend Manker had the latter two exhumed and, indeed, found arsenic in both their stomachs. Rather eerily, the last article I could find said that although she was still under suspicion, Jane had been made the administrator of her murdered sister's estate, which included the insurance money for the infant daughter she left behind. Oh, that doesn't sound good at all.

If anyone knows more about Jane, please let me know.

I am often asked if I have a favorite case. Yes, there are many. Catharine Schumacher Sharp Batchelor Reiff intrigues me; I would like to have met her. I feel sorry for Sue Beaver and wish I knew more about her, but her death became more about the men involved than about this redheaded blue-eyed girl, the mistress of a wealthy, married banker.

My heart breaks for Madge Augustine Oberholtzer who was brutally raped by the man who ruled Indiana in the 1920s—the Grand Dragon of the Ku Klux Klan. The evil of Belle Gunness, listed as one of the most prolific murderers in the Guinness Book of World Records, is frightening and overwhelming. We know she killed at least 40 people—some estimates put it as high as 180—in the pretty lakeside town of La Porte.

Jennie Olsen's sweetheart was told she was going to California, but she ended up in Belle's backyard. Photo courtesy of the La Porte County Historical Society.

On Valentine's Day 1923, bootlegger Harry Diamond shot his wife and tried to blame it on their chauffeur. Photo courtesy of the Indiana State Archives.

I wonder about Luella Mabbitt. Was she murdered or did she really run away? I'm guessing the latter. I hope she met a nice man after her lover was lynched. I don't think she moved to Mexico; I think she really ended up in New York.

And I wish Pearl Bryan had gotten on the train that day when she sat in the station trying to decide what to do. She should have gone back home to Greencastle, had her baby, and met a nice young man. It would have saved her head, which was never found.

I didn't write this book alone. I had so much exceptional help from Karen Rettinger, the archive manager at the Marshall County Historical Society, who took the little bit of knowledge I had about the Susan Beaver case and helped bring her story to light. The same is true of Eva Lindsay of the Spencer County Public Library; Tony Collignon, president of the Perry County Historical Society; and archivists at Indiana University's Lilly Library who were able to locate long-forgotten documents on Catharine Batchelor, growing her story from just a small town beauty handy with the poison vial known as Indiana's Lucretia Borgia into more. The staff at the La Porte County Historical Society were fantastic as well, taking the time out of a busy day to provide photos and coroner transcripts—yes, I am the type who spends time reading those.

Joan Hostetler, as always, I enjoyed talking to and sharing historic gossip with. Though she is planning to write a book about Rufus Cantrell, the King of Ghouls, she was still willing to share anecdotes about his work as a resurrection man.

Putnam County Historian Larry Tiffin was wonderful, taking time to gather photos of Greencastle where Pearl Bryan grew up; so was Jan Lester, a volunteer, at Campbell County Historical and Genealogical Society.

For those who tirelessly and anonymously digitalize old court transcripts; legal documents; birth, marriage, and death records; and take snapshots and write histories for Find-A-Grave, I offer a big shout out. Writing a book like this would be, at least for me, nearly impossible without all those long, dusty hours of effort.

Preserving history and passing it on is a wonderful gift for all those in the past, present, and future.

Thanks also to Ashley Runyon, the acquisitions editor at Indiana University Press, who suggested this book. If she hadn't done so, I never would have met all the people who decades ago were front page news and have now passed mostly into obscurity. I am so glad I got the chance to tell their stories.

MURDERS

THAT MADE HEADLINES

1

CATHARINE SCHUMAKER: AN INDIANA LUCRETIA BORGIA

Jasper Weekly Courier, Friday, June 23, 1871

Even those who believed she had poisoned two husbands and one inconvenient wife described Catharine Schumaker as "very beautiful with sparkling eyes, black and as bright as polished jet; her form was faultless, her carriage graceful, her conversation animated and vivacious" wrote a seemingly smitten reporter for the *Jasper Weekly Courier.*

The daughter of a German farmer, her family had immigrated first to Louisville, Kentucky, and then to Rockport, Indiana, from Baden, Germany, when Catharine was just two. When she was around fifteen, Catharine, whose last name is sometimes listed as Melchior, Shoemaker, and Schumacher (the German version of *shoemaker*), went to work for Mathias and Mary Sharp, an elderly couple who owned a large and prosperous farm a few miles outside of Rockport.

"Mr. Sharp and his aged wife lived alone together their children having all married and removed from the homestead," reported the February 8, 1872, edition of the *Louisville Ledger* in an article titled, predictably enough, "A Lucretia Borgia." "The old people were highly esteemed and were known to nearly all the citizens of the county."

MATHIAS SHARP HOUSE
CIRCA 1867
This house was built by Mathias and Katherine Sharp on property once owned by Judge John Pitcher, Spencer County's first lawyer and Abraham Lincoln's close friend. It was the first house in Rockport to be designed by an architect and the first bluff house to be built with the front facing the river. Mathias died here from poisoning as did Katherine's second husband. Katherine was later prosecuted for the poisonings. Some believe the ghost of the two men still inhabit the house.
In 1877 the noted ichthyologist Dr. Carl H. Eigenman came here to reside with his uncle, the prominent Rockport businessman, Capt. John Eigenman.

NATIONAL REGISTER OF HISTORIC PLACES   1983

Mathias Sharp built this beautiful home on the Ohio River for his much younger wife, Catharine, and then, after making a new will in her favor, he became sick and died. Photo courtesy of Rockport Mayor Gay Ann Harney.

This paper too was entranced with Catharine's looks, describing her almost breathlessly as "a beautiful woman, with faultless form and graceful motion—a woman who would attract attention wherever she went."

Making herself very useful to the elderly couple in many ways, Catharine helped nurse Mary Sharp when she began suffering intense abdominal pains that doctors seemed helpless to treat. Mrs. Sharp died on February 9, 1855, and Catharine, so close to her employer, was emotionally distraught according to contemporary accounts—or so it seemed. Later, it would be said that the symptoms were very much like those of arsenic or strychnine poisoning, but at the time, Mary's death wasn't questioned, and poor Mrs. Sharp was buried and seemingly soon forgotten.

Catharine remained with Mathias, earning a generous salary for not only running his home but also as the general superintendent of the domestic division of his extensive farm. The grief of the widower, forty-four years Catharine's senior, dissipated quickly and he soon began courting the teenaged girl seemingly giving truth to the old saying "there's no fool like an old fool."

Young, beautiful, and always in demand, Catharine hesitated. It could be she wasn't sure whether she wanted to marry such an old man. But then again, Sharp was one of the richest available men around. He had moved to Southern Indiana from New Jersey shortly after the War of 1812, buying up a vast stretch of fertile land on the Ohio River just a few miles from what would become the city of Rockport, which was laid out in 1818. Besides farming, he also most likely speculated in land, and his earnings enabled him to hire a Cincinnati artist to paint portraits of both Mary and himself, to help plank roads for easier travel, and to invest in the founding of a private school.

He might be a fool about love, but certainly, at least before he met Catharine, not about money.

According to a rather racy and clearly embellished article in the *Nashville Union and American* published on Saturday, February 10, 1872, Catharine argued that marrying Mathias "would be too much like uniting June with December." But as she said these words, "she looked up languishingly from her lustrous black eyes and beautiful face into the face of her aged lover. Those glances, as she well knew, were not to be withstood and so the old man's passion was only inflamed and his suit pressed with more earnest determination."

Though the *Union and American* reporter likely took some journalistic license in the scenes he described—after all he probably wasn't there—there was some truth in his reporting. For the winning of her hand in marriage, Catharine was able to negotiate the deed to Sharp's farm said to be the most valuable in Spencer County and valued in today's monetary terms at about $900,000 (see, told you he was rich). She also asked for $1,000 in cash, an amount equivalent to about $28,000 today.

Mary and Mathias had several living children at the time and many more grandchildren who must have been dismayed at the thought of losing their inheritance. But that didn't stop Mathias from, excuse the pun, giving away the farm. But Catharine wanted even more. Besides the land and the cash, the other big "get" for Catharine was a home in Rockport.

And why not? Beautiful and now rich, what young woman would want to stay on a farm even if it was the best in Spencer County? Rockport, on the Ohio River, was a major traffic route at a time when traveling by land along, depending on the season, muddy or dusty and rutted earthen roads, was a dirty and slow way to go. Boats loaded with goods and passengers came into the city daily, and the city's bustling taverns, grain and grist mills, restaurants, and shops were open for business. Catharine could treat herself to all sorts of things at stores such as G. J. Hales, seller of lady's fancy goods; Simon Greenbaum's jewelry store; T. C. Tuft's boots and shoes; and J. & A. Kersteins furniture store. Close to the city, she wouldn't need to rely on what was grown on the farm, but instead she could visit any of the many grocers such as those owned by James Turpin, G. B. Bullock, Isaac Gillette, and J. J. Cavin. For pastries, there were German bakers such as H. Langmesser and Jacob Eigenmann. For sundries there were apothecary choices including Samuel Turner and Oliver Morgan and dry good emporiums with names such as Hurst, De Bruler & Sharp, J. T. Morgan, Joseph Shoenfeld, and Stewart & Shrode.

If at this time Catharine didn't know the location of the shop belonging to S. B. Thompson, a cabinet maker and, as was common back then, undertaker, she most likely soon would. She'd be purchasing a few of his coffins.

Like the farm and the cash, Mathias seemed to be all in for a new house in town overlooking the river. Reaching an agreement regarding all of Catharine's demands, the papers were drawn up and the marriage took place on December 22, 1855, a little over ten months after the death of Sharp's first wife.

Evening Star (Washington, DC), Tuesday, February 13, 1872

> For a couple of years or more the infatuated old man bathed in the sunshine of her smiles and received her toying with all the delight of a child.

A Cincinnati architect was said to have designed the grand home the Sharps built on Third Street in Rockport. With its river views, the couple could sit on their porch and watch the boats, ferries, and skiffs navigate the river. Still standing all these years later, the brick Italianate-style house features eight fireplaces with iron mantles, a two-story central pavilion, two wings with bay windows, a walnut staircase leading up to the second floor, and ornate porches. Now on the National Register of Historic Places, it was completed in 1867. Two years later, Mathias wrote his last will. No matter the manner of his death, the will was very generous to Catharine not only for being such a kindly and caring spouse but also in spite of the bitterness of his adult children toward their young stepmother.

Mathias Sharp: Last Will and Testament

In the name of the Benevolent Father of All, Amen! I, Mathias Sharp of Spencer County, Indiana being weak in body, advanced in years but of sound (illegible), mind and memory, do make and publish this my last will and testament hereby revoking and making void all other wills by me at any time heretofore made.

Item 1st, I desire that as soon as is possible after my death that my just debts and funeral expenses be paid by my executors here in after namely out of the first monies that may come into their hands, and I desire my funeral to be conducted in a manner suitable to my condition in life.

Item 2nd, I give and bequeath unto my beloved wife Catharine Sharp all my household and kitchen furniture of every nature and description. Together with my horses, carriage, wagon and other loose property about the barn. Also five hundred dollars in money. And the real estate with all the upper ten acres thereof named and described in a Deed of Conveyance by me to her under date of November 12th, 1866.

Mathias willed other property to Catharine and also left $500 each to Gerhardt and Edmund Sharp, the sons of his brother John. These amounts were to be paid to the boys by Catharine when they turned twenty-one. In the meantime, she was allowed to collect the interest on the sums. The heirs of Morris Sharp and Arthur Sharp, the deceased sons of Mathias and Mary, would get a third of the remainder of his estate. His two daughters, Eliza Sargent and Anne Hammond, inherited a third each.

As for who would handle his estate, toward the end of the document, written in a neat cursive penmanship, Mathias states: "I hereby nominate and appoint my wife Catharine Sharp and R. J. Hicks executors of my last will and testament and earnestly request them to carry out this will in letter and spirit."

It was dated August 18, 1869.

Before the end of the year, with the house completed and the will filed, Mathias suddenly took ill, suffering acute stomach pains similar to those Mary Sharp had suffered in the last few months of her life. The story is he died at the kitchen table, and the cause of death is listed as dyspepsia. It would be said later that Catharine's second husband died at the same table of the same illness (more about that husband later—though he appears to have actually died in bed).

Not surprisingly, Mathias and Mary's children were unhappy with the terms of the will. Insidious rumors soon circulated about the manner of his death. "His children and many of his neighbors believed that both he (Mathias Sharp) and his first wife had died from poison at the hands of Catharine, but they never dared only breath the suspicions in suppression of whispers, lest the law should take hold of them in the shape of an action for slander."

A beguiling rich woman with a fabulous house, you can figure Catharine wasn't lonely for long. On August 17, 1870, Samuel T. Batchelor and Catharine Sharp took out a marriage license. A widower, Batchelor had married his first wife, Frances Fuguay, who was born April 16, 1843, on July 13, 1867, in nearby Warwick, Indiana. Fannie, as she was known, died on February 5, 1869. The couple's son, Willie, born in 1868, died the same year as his mother though the exact date isn't known. Fannie rests at Castle Cemetery in Newburgh, another river city along the Ohio, next to other members of her family. The etching on her tombstone depicts a fist clutching a bouquet of wilting flowers, the symbol of a life cut too short.

Who was the lucky groom? Some newspaper accounts describe Sam as a successful businessman with good looks and good health. A few newspapers, including the *Rockport Democrat,* which was decidedly pro-Catharine, give a gloomier view of her choice.

"Something after a year's widowhood she was wooed and won by Mr. Batchelor, who was a sickly man with a broken down constitution. He died about eight months after his marriage with Mrs. Sharp. He was not a merchant but was clerking in the stores of Messrs. Lemmon and Taylor; nor had he any property whatever at the date of his marriage with Mrs. Sharp."

In other words, Sam was a loser and not deserving of such a prize. Batchelor, whether or not well-to-do, was definitely much younger than Mathias, and contemporary news accounts describe the newly married couple as seemingly devoted to each other. During the time of their short marriage, something happened to impel the Sharp family beyond whispered suspicions and in September 1871, determined to get back what they saw as rightfully theirs, they filed a motion in civil court in Spencer County. What emboldened them is unclear, but newspaper accounts say that they managed to wrest some of their father's property away from Catharine by saying she had undue influence over Mathias. Liza Sharp also filed a lawsuit against both Catharine and Sam but the outcome isn't known.

BUT SUDDENLY HE DIED

Evening Star (**Washington, DC**), **Tuesday, February 13, 1872**

> His disease was a languishing one at first, and indicated towards its fatal termination a speedy recovery. But those dreadful pains which had been noticed in the illness of his wife immediately prior to her demise supervened and as suddenly and painfully as his aged wife had died so did he. His children and many of his neighbors believed that both he and his first wife had died from poison at the hands of Catharine, but they dared only briefed their suspicions in suppressed whispers, lest the law should take hold of them in the shape for an action for slander. Catharine was rich. She had but just reached the prime of womanhood, was THE MOST BEAUTIFUL WOMAN IN THE COUNTY.

Nashville Union and American, **Saturday, February 10, 1872**

> But after a year or two of bliss, Mr. Bachelor was attacked by a languishing illness which increased and diminished by turns until the disease, which puzzled the skill of the physicians, took a favorable turn and strong hopes were entertained for its speedy and favorable termination. It was a noticeable feature of Mr. Batchelor's disease, as it had been of the disease of Mr. Sharp and his first wife had died, that it was seated in the stomach and no medicines seemed to control it. His partial recovery was therefore unaccountable to the physician upon any other hypothesis that the great physical recuperative powers of Mr. Batchelor. But in the midst of the fond anticipations of his friends for his recovery, Mr. Batchelor suddenly died in great agony, suffering intense pain in the stomach.

Rich or poor, Batchelor, who died April 12, 1871, was a Master Mason and his fellow freemasons were determined to find out if he'd been murdered.

> The ever vigilant members of the order were not willing that their brother should thus perish without avenging his death. So

they had his body disinterred, the stomach taken out and sent to Dr. Jenkins of Louisville for analyzation of its contents and the analysis developed the existence of sufficient strychnine to produce death. . . . The Mason fraternity had the murderess arrested and her commitment in bonds of $15,000 to answer the crime. . . . Ten years ago we knew the woman as one among the most beautiful and respected ladies in Spencer County. Such are life's deceptions and uncertainties.

Jasper Weekly Courier, **Friday, June 23, 1871**

The stomach traveled in a jar by boat as Rockport druggist Aurelius D. Garlinghouse would later testify. Garlinghouse was in attendance when Batchelor was exhumed (it's hard to tell from reading the news accounts whether this was an official act or one that his friends and fellow Masons took upon themselves to do) and saw the organ placed in a jar. The jar was "then carried by Dr. Morgan to Mr. Basye's drug store in Rockport and in company with Dr. Morgan conveyed to Louisville; delivered to Dr. Thomas Jenkins; took his receipt for it and returned home."

Convinced that Batchelor wasn't the only husband treated like a rat, the *Evansville Courier* reported that on receiving word that strychnine was found in Batchelor's stomach, suspicions arose about Mathias Sharp's death. The digging up of bodies became popular and soon Mathias was out of the ground (no one seems to have bothered with bringing Mary back to the surface) and his stomach removed. It was taken by Captain Adams aboard the steamship *Mary Ameld* to Evansville where it was delivered to the Evansville Medical College and turned over to the medical facility there. Some papers reported that it too tested positive, though no charges were made against Catharine, while others said no poison was found. Maybe the seventy-four-year-old Sharp really did just die of dyspepsia, though in those days before refrigeration and good preservation systems, it could have been food poisoning as well.

It had to be a relief for Catharine. She had only one murder charge to deal with.

Catharine was called in front of a grand jury; the result wasn't good.

> Now comes the Grand Jury and returns into court the following bills of Indictment. The State of Indiana versus Catharine Batchelor: Murder in the First Degree.
>
> Now here the Bail of the defendant in this case is fixed by the County at fifteen thousand dollars.

Catharine pled not guilty to the charges, and her lawyers filed an affidavit for a change of venue "on account of local passions and biased opinions."

Calvin Jones, the editor and proprietor of the *Rockport Democrat* was definitely on Catharine's side, lambasting the *Louisville Ledger* as joining the many of Rockport who had turned against her.

A FINE ROMANCE SPOILED—FACTS AND FICTION

Rockport Democrat, **Saturday, February 17, 1872**

> The idea that because a poor defenseless [all who think Catharine was defenseless, raise their hands] female is so unfortunate as to have been left a widow and because she lived conceived the notion that she was a bad woman and therefore every libeler in the land should slander and traduce the victim of what is believed by many good people as a conspiracy not only against the good name but against the life of a lady who for 20 years was an exemplary church member and an honest God fearing woman.

The court agreed with both Calvin and Catharine and the trial moved to Perry County.

Husbandless and without the resources to afford the best defense, Catharine sought help from John Eigenman to help pay for her defense. German-born like many who settled in Rockford, including Catharine and her family, Eigenman was injured and held captive during the Civil War when fighting for the Union Army. Upon returning to Rockport, he worked again as a builder and contractor and was the owner of Pearl Mills, which produced grain, feed, and flour. In exchange for $15,000, Catharine deeded him the house Mathias had left her. Eigenman and then his son would live there until 1900.

But she also had a phalanx of stalwart men in her life as she readied for court including her brother Christopher Schumaker, Baiser Romig, Adam Long, John Koch, August Euler, and her brother-in-law John Biedenkopf, all described as "honest, upright and hardworking German citizens of Spencer County."

Though she lost her house, Catharine used the money wisely. When her case came to trial in Cannelton, a mill town on the Ohio River in Perry County, she was represented by Charles Denby, Hatfield & Peckinpaugh, and G. E. Bullock, a well-respected law firm.

THE BATCHELOR POISONING CASE

First Day Proceedings

Rockport Weekly Democrat, March 9, 1872

Court started at 8:30 a.m. with the Honorable D. T. Laird on the bench. The state was represented by Circuit Prosecutor C. A. DeBruler, Esq., and by Hon. L. Q. DeBruler. The appearance of Catharine Batchelor, on entering the courtroom, was impressive and calculated to inspire feelings of sympathy and compassion.

"The lady is about 30 years old, of medium height and gracefully developed," wrote a reporter. "She has a pleasant face, keen black eyes and a fine suite of hair."

The Killing Business

The defense, cross-examining Dr. White who had treated Samuel during his final days, wrung the following testimony from him. White's conclusion was that Samuel, who had been building a barn, took a cold by sitting on some lumber.

> I do not know but little of his general health when I was called upon to visit him. I found him in bed; he had something like congestion of the stomach. I went to see him regularly until he died; I

prescribed the medicines administered to him myself; the drugs were procured at the drug store of Mr. John Basye; I never analyzed any of them during; during my treatment I gave him calomel, bicarbonate of soda, morphine and bicarbonate of potash.

The symptoms White observed were typical of those for tetanus such as muscle spasms, lockjaw, and spasms with arched back and neck. Seeing Batchelor with his head turned back and his arms pulled back from his body, White ordered a mustard plaster and left the room, and when he got back, Batchelor had breathed his last.

Though White's testimony about tetanus (and Batchelor had been working on building a barn so he probably would have been around rusty nails and other metals) didn't implicate Catharine, the testimonies of the other witnesses called by the prosecution were extremely damaging to her case.

Evansville Journal, **Saturday Morning, March 9, 1872**

My name is Jesse White Kinchcloe. I live in Rockport; was acquainted with Mr. Batchelor during his life; am acquainted with Mrs. Batchelor and sold strychnine to her; she bought strychnine the day before her husband died. I asked her if she was going into the killing business. She said she was going to kill some rats. I prepared it; put it in a paper. That was the day before Mr. Batchelor died; I suppose it was between nine and ten o'clock in the morning.

During the cross-examination by the defense, Kinchcloe said he never measured strychnine except for prescriptions.

"I prepared it and she paid me ten cents," he said.

It seems that Catharine had a lot of rats on her property, because she bought even more strychnine. Garlinghouse, the same Rockport druggist and fellow Mason who helped in the midnight exhumation of Batchelor's body, testified he sold Catharine five cents worth of strychnine on April 3.

"I am acquainted with Catharine Batchelor," he testified. "She called at our drug store for strychnine. I asked what she wanted with it; she said to kill rats. I said to her arsenic was better; she said she had been used to using strychnine and I put it up for her."

But probably the most damning testimony came from Rockport resident B. M. Taylor, Sam's employer at a mercantile store, who had been at the house during the days before Sam's death. He was there on Monday and Tuesday nights, and Batchelor had told him he was getting better. On Wednesday, he was back at the house in a sitting room connected to a bedroom whose door was ajar. Taylor testified in court:

> I could see, therefore, from the position I had, see everything that was going on in the bedroom. While in this position I saw Mrs. B. go to the bureau, unlock the drawer, take a small package out and then lock it again and put the key in her pocket. She then put part of the package into a spoon, went to the bed, put her left arm under Batchelor's head, raised him up and gave him the drug., whatever it was. . . . I remained some ten or fifteen minutes after the drug was administered and then left.
>
> Went back that night with Mr. Laird and Kercheval; when I got back, Mr. Batchelor was dead.

The trial, which lasted three days and had an all-male jury (women couldn't vote or serve on a jury back then), attracted a crowd that included a large number of women—a common occurrence in murder cases back then involving a female defendant and one that almost inevitably elicited a strong editorial or two in the local newspapers fuming about how women should be home with their children instead of in a courtroom.

And so it was with Catharine. The March 2, 1872, edition of the *Cannelton Reporter* reported that when the jury returned in a few minutes with a verdict of "not guilty," the onlookers congratulated Catharine on her acquittal.

The closing speeches delivered by her attorneys were described as being extremely artful, logical, forcible, and eloquent. "The flashes of pathos, wit and piercing sarcasm, impassioned philosophy, swept everything before them like the Chicago Fire," is how it was written up in the 1885 edition of "History of Warrick, Spencer, and Perry Counties, Indiana: from the earliest time to the present; together with interesting biographical sketches, reminiscences, notes, etc."

But who might have helped Catharine even more was presiding Judge Laird. After the jury announced their verdict, he showed himself as anything but impartial, vehemently saying, "I wasn't going to have a woman hanged just because of what a damned expert with a kettle of guts said. . . . That woman is my neighbor. . . . I keep my cow in her barn."

Even after two widowhoods and well into what then would have been middle age, Catharine retained the charm that had garnered her a fortune and, eventually, three marriages.

Having been saved from prison or hanging, on June 19, 1875, Catharine married Frederick G. Reiff a well-established landowner in nearby Grandville. Like Catharine's other two husbands, Reiff was a widower. His wife Margaret Miller Reiff, born August 3, 1837, died on January 28, 1875, less than six months before the Batchelor-Reiff wedding. She is buried at Sunset Hill Cemetery in Rockport.

Reiff, who like Catharine was born in Germany, might be considered a brave man for marrying a woman thought to have murdered three people. But time would show there was no need to worry. The couple stayed together until his death in 1914; Catharine died five years later on August 9, 1919 (the same month and day as her birth). She was eighty-three years old and in her will she bequeathed her estate to her stepson, Charles W. Reiff of Spencer County, Indiana "for his kindness and services to me in the past and in attention to me in the future." She made an "x" where her name should have been, most likely meaning she hadn't learned to write.

The couple had been married for almost forty years, a remarkable period of time even now, but more so in rural Indiana in the 1800s.

If Catharine didn't murder her former husbands and one—or maybe more—inconvenient wives, it would be nice to believe that she found contentment after so narrowly escaping death.

Suspected of three murders, including those of two husbands and an inconvenient wife, Catharine Shumacher Sharp Batcher Reiff lived to the grand age of eighty-three. Photo courtesy of Find-A-Grave.

But Catharine's story doesn't end there. If ghost stories are to be believed—and there are plenty—she continued to long for her grand home on the Ohio River in Rockport. When the Posey family bought what is still known, even 150 or so years later, as the Mathias Sharp house, there were stories of it being haunted, by both a woman and a man (Mathias? Sam?). The most intriguing tale recounts how one day, Mrs. Posey and her daughters, who were sitting on the front porch, saw a frail old woman garbed in a long black dress walking up the drive toward them. As she drew closer, they could hear her saying over and over again, "They robbed me of this place. They robbed me of this place."

Was it Catharine's ghost? The Poseys didn't think so, they thought it was the real Catharine come back to the place she loved.

Whether it was Catharine in the flesh or her ghostly apparition depends on when they saw this woman dressed in black. The Poseys purchased the house in 1913, six years before Catharine died. If she appeared during those years, yes it was Catharine who according to records lived nearby in Grandview. But if the lady approached the house after 1919, it could only have been her ghost.

Author's note: Was Catharine guilty? Deaths were frequent back then and both Mathias and Mary were elderly and medical care wasn't exactly at its zenith. (Mustard plasters to treat tetanus?) She did buy a lot of rat poison shortly before Sam died, and his employer claimed to see Catharine take a box from a locked drawer and feed it to her husband. That testimony raises several questions: Why would he concoct such a story? But then again, why would the capable Catharine, if she had decided to murder Batchelor, not have been more careful? She could have at least shut the door. Catharine as a cold and calculating poisoner seems much more believable than Catharine as a clueless and careless woman.

Also, there are the three wives—Mary, Fannie and Margaret. Did Catharine conveniently get rid of her rivals? Mary was elderly and Fannie possibly died in childbirth as her young son died that same year. As for Margaret, no death record was located so the reason for her passing is unknown. None of the many articles about

Catharine imply that she murdered Fannie and Margaret. There may have been talk but we'll probably never know.

Contemporary accounts at the time reported that Catharine was extremely upset when Mary died and again when Mathias passed away (though there was no such description of her emotional state regarding Batchelor's death). Was it guilt or genuine grief? As for her last marriage, were the two happy? If she didn't murder her former husbands and one—or maybe more—inconvenient wives, we wish her the best.

Unfortunately all is most likely lost to time. Unless, that is, we happen upon her ghost outside the house Mathias built for her.

2

An Unfortunate Indiana Family: Minnie May and Luella Mabbitt

THE HISTORY OF TWO GREAT CRIMES IN
ONE FAMILY: THE MABBITT TRIAL

*The Mabbitts Come of Good Old Farmer
Stock, Now Sorely Tried by Sorrow*

———————

*The Hideous Wrongs Committed against
Their Daughters—Minnie's Infant Drowned,
for Which She Is Now Being Tried*

———————

*Scenes in the Crowded Courtroom—The Selection
of the Jury—Pleas Entered by the Attorneys of the
Accused—Defendant's Aged Parents Present*

Indianapolis News, **Tuesday, February 24, 1891**

The infanticide trial of pretty Minnie Mabbitt didn't really begin
when Joseph F. Jenkins, marshal of West Indianapolis, found the
body of an infant in Eagle Creek in Indianapolis in 1890. Instead,
it stretched back to August 1886 when her beautiful older sister,
Luella Mabbitt, disappeared late one night.

Luella had been courted by Amer Green, but because of her father's disapproval of the match and at his insistence, she wrote Green a note ending their relationship.

A few days later she would disappear.

It happened on the night when William Walker, who was courting Luella's twin sister Ella, rode up to the house and called for her to come out, which she did. As they stood chatting, Green showed up and started shouting for Luella to come outside as well. When told she was sleeping, Green became angry, saying if she didn't come down, he'd "tear the house apart. Therefore Luella got up and went out to him and talked a while, then they started off together, apparently, for a walk. Walker drove off in his horse and buggy and the sister returned to the house. That was the last ever seen of Luella alive. It was claimed that cries were heard along the road leading towards Wildcat Creek south, but no attention was paid to them."

Carroll County, Indiana, Archives History, 1916

Another variation of what happened that evening has Amer arriving at the Mabbitt home in a jealous rage, abducting Luella, and driving her off in his carriage. He was not seen again until morning when he arrived at his own home, alone, abandoned the carriage, and then left again.

At the time of Luella's disappearance, the Mabbitts, a wealthy and long-established farm family, lived just south of Delphi, Indiana, on the banks of Wildcat Creek, a tributary to the Wabash River. The daughters were all popular, bright, and pretty, but Luella was considered the prettiest of all (Minnie would earn that honor in a few years) and her disappearance caused anguish and anger in the community.

A lynch mob formed, a not uncommon occurrence in Indiana back then, and rode to the Green home. Convinced that Green's mother knew the whereabouts of her son, the mob tossed a rope around the woman's neck, threatening to kill her unless she revealed

Historic downtown Delphi has many of the same buildings that Luella and Minnie Mabbitt would have frequented when they lived there more than a century ago. Photo courtesy of Jane Simon Ammeson.

where he was. If she knew, she refused to tell, and the crowd didn't carry out their threat but instead rode away. However, someone had to pay so Mrs. Green was arrested and jailed along with William Walker who had the misfortune of being at the Mabbitt home on the night Luella vanished.

Besides her son, Amer, being suspected of murder, Mrs. Green had other heartaches as well. Her other son had murdered Enos Brumbaught (also sometimes spelled Brunsbaugh) and he, too, had left the state. Agents of the Pinkerton Detective Agency were on the trail of both of the Green boys—Amer was suspected of helping his brother escape. The detectives tracked Amer and William to Texas but by then they had moved on and were said to be in Kansas. As for Mrs. Green, she was released from jail, and like her sons, decided that Indiana wasn't the place to be so she moved to Ohio. The Mabbitts had also hired detectives to find Luella, but if she were alive or dead, no one was able to locate her.

As for Amer and William, there are two stories as to what happened next. Some say Deputy Sherriff Buck Stanley apprehended the two in Texas. Another tale says the Pinkertons staked out Mrs. Green's Ohio home and caught the brothers when they came to visit. The first is probably true as Amer Green would later tell a mob intent on lynching him that he had attempted to tell Stanley the truth when he came to Fort Worth, Texas to arrest him.

In February 1887, six months after Luella disappeared, a badly decomposed body, described as almost unrecognizable, was pulled from the Wabash River. Ella Mabbitt and her parents viewed the body and said it was indeed Luella. On February 11, they testified at the coroner's inquest in Lafayette that the remains of the woman found in the river the previous Sunday were those of Luella Mabbitt because the teeth resembled those of her sister Ella.

The Adams Mill Covered Bridge spans Wildcat Creek. On the night Luella Mabbitt disappeared, people reported hearing cries from near the creek. Photo courtesy of Jane Simon Ammeson.

The Adams Mill uses water from Wildcat Creek to grind grain as it did back when the Mabbitts lived here. Clothes found near the creek were said to belong to Luella Mabbitt. Photo courtesy of Jane Simon Ammeson.

AMER GREEN LYNCHED

A Masked Mob Hang the Abductor of Luella Mabbitt

Walnut Grove, Delphi, the Scene of the Violence—
The Helpless Victim Maintains His Innocence

Indianapolis News, **Saturday, October 22, 1887**

Green had just barely escaped being lynched shortly after Luella disappeared. In October 1887, Buck Stanley, deputy sheriff of Cass County who was also as an evangelist, tracked Amer Green to southwestern Texas and brought him back first to the Michigan City prison where he was taken for his own protection and then, because of his upcoming trial, to the Carroll County jail. When news of his capture and imprisonment became known, it was noted that strangers were appearing on the street but no one seemed to give it much mind.

AMER GREEN FALLS A VICTIM
TO THEIR WRATH AT DELPHI

Chicago Tribune, **Saturday, October 22, 1887**

At about midnight tonight those of our citizens who happened to be on the streets were startled by the appearance of a large body of men making their way into the city. It needed no second glance to tell that they were bound on a mission of death. Quietly they made their way to the county jail, and after stationing guards to each avenue approaching they proceeded to break in the doors of the Sheriff's residence. That official was awakened by the crash of timbers as the doors were crushed in, and came out, when the leader of the mob demanded the keys to the prison. The Sheriff refused to deliver them and he was taken in hand by other members of the organization.

A sledgehammer was then brought forward, and after a few hard blows the locks dropped to the floor. Entering the mob rushed directly up-stairs to the cell-rooms and made an attack on the locks there. It required some time to break the combination by which the cells were locked, but once at the levers the leader reached in and pulled one which opened the cell containing Amer Green, the abductor and murderer of Luella Mabbitt. The prisoner was gruffly ordered to get up and dress, which he mechanically did, and he was pushed forward at the muzzle of a cocked revolver. When the outside was reached he was placed in a covered wagon in deadness and the crowd moved off.

The mob consisted of 180 men, all armed. The men made little attempt to disguise themselves. Each wore a handkerchief over the lower part of his face. In addition to the regularly organized mob a crowd of probably 100 men was near at hand. Before reaching the city the avengers had tied their horses on the outskirts and proceeded into the city with nothing but the wagon in which the murderer was placed.

Green, a giant of a man according to those who knew him, had tried to protect himself by wrenching a large piece of water pipe from the wall of his cell, but he was no match for the crowd. Green was seized, tied up, pushed into a double-seated covered carriage, and then driven at breakneck speed east on the Delphi and Flora roads. Crossing Deer Creek bridge, the carriage stopped when it reached the top of the hill and was soon joined by about sixty carriages, buggies, wagons, and horseback riders. "Some of the mob remarked that they would torture Green and make him confess. Green realized that his time had come, and maintained the stolid indifference which had characterized him since he was captured. The mob was composed of Cass and Carroll County men and their determined manner left no doubt that they intended to forever settle question as to Amer Green's fate."

The procession moved on to Walnut Grove, about eight miles southeast where two large bonfires, burning bright, illuminated the woods.

Green remained cool and calm according to the newspaper reporter who was at the scene. "He towered above his captors, a helpless victim," wrote the reporter. "In a few minutes after the fatal spot reached, after he had been placed near the fire."

Asked if Luella Mabbitt was alive, Green said, "She is. She's at Fort Worth, Texas living with Samuel Payne."

Then, sensing the inevitability of the moment, he added, "I hope you are not going to burn me; you have come out to murder me, and are going to do it, but do it like civilized men."

The mob wasn't in the mood for mercy, many cried out, "Give him the stake." "Burn him." "Torture a confession out of him."

Amer was next asked why Luella, if she were still alive, didn't come home.

"She would if I had the time to send for her," he replied.

"Why did she not come back and relieve her distressed father and mother?" another asked.

"She was scared and at the same time angry," says Amer. "She said she would not come back. She said she would starve or die in the poor house rather than come back. We had arranged to go away for a long time before we went. Once when we went to Kokomo she wanted to run away but I had no money and we could not go. The night we went, Luella had arranged for it; she had taken some of her clothing down to the barn and she got it when we went away."

Green was asked what William Walker, who had barely escaped lynching, knew about their discussions, and Green replied Walker didn't know anything about them.

He took Luella to Frankfort and then drove to Kokomo to get money to go away.

"We met in Indianapolis and went away together," Green told the large group of men who were intent, no matter what, on murdering him. "She is still alive."

"It's a lie. Choke the truth out of him," came from the crowd.

"I won't satisfy you," said Green. "There is no use talking to you. You have decided to murder me. The most absurd stories have been told, and now that hair that was found in my trunk in Tascoosa. It was foolish to think that the hair of Luella Mabbitt. Buck Stanley told me that and said it was her hair. It was not. I'd have explained this all at Fort

Worth, if Buck Stanley would have permitted me. I sent for my attorney then but Stanley hustled me away became he came to see me. I had no chance or I'd have produced her there. Buck Stanley will tell you that."

Green was correct in stating the mob, many of them people he knew, were determined to kill him and no amount of logic or reasoning would change that. They wouldn't even give him time to ask Luella to come home to save him.

Then he asked whether Mr. Mabbitt was in the crowd.

"Yes," responded the crowd.

"Let him step forwards," said the leader of the mob.

The old gray-haired father of the missing girl moved to the front and in the glare of the flickering light stood.

Face to Face with Amer Green

Well Amer, you must now tell the truth. You must tell me what you did with my dear girl. You took her away from her home and have kept her away. What did you do with her?

"I loved her better than my own life and that is the reason I went away with her," he said. "I loved her better than you did and all the times she has been away I have cared for her."

William Mabbitt would later deny he was a member of the crowd, but others, including reporters, said that not only was he there but so were his sons Oris and Mont and his brother. Both boys were later tried for murder. Indeed, Mont, whose real name was the rather interesting one of Montezuma, later boasted that he was the one who placed the noose around Amer's neck.

One reporter wrote, "The fire in the grove flickered and cast weird shadows on the ground while the stars, so calm and beautiful, looked down from a cloudless sky. The fearful tragedy that was about to be enacted presented an awful nature, for nature was at rest." Someone scrambled up the walnut tree to tie the rope and then it was placed around Amer's neck as he stood in the wagon seat.

"Are you an innocent man?" asked the *Journal* reporter, who had stood a mute spectator of the mob's dread work.

"I am an innocent man."

"What is your last request?" continued the newspaperman.

"That you inform my mother, send her my body and tell her I desire to buried by the side of my sister in Ohio."

"At Hebron, Ohio?"

"Yes, and . . ."

Here the horses gave a lurch forward and Amer Green was suspended between earth and sky.

When the body fell, the rope seemed to stretch four feet and it looked as if the victim would touch the ground. The rope was strong however and there was a least three feet between the soles of his boots and the ground. He never moved muscle after the fall. It was thought his neck was broken. As his body swung in space all was quiet and in a few minutes the original crowd quietly dispersed. As we go to press the body is still hanging and it will probably not be disturbed until the coroner takes charge of it.

Those who witnessed the execution and started home met scores of vehicles making for the grove. The word had gone out and the whole country is aroused. Thousands of people will visit the spot today.

There was plenty of time for gawking at Amer's body as the body remained hanging from the walnut tree until the coroner took charge of it the next day. The court ordered a grand jury be convened and more than one hundred witnesses were questioned, but no one could identify even one of the participants in the lynching.

A famed photograph, still available online, shows Amer, his neck at an angle, hanging from a tree in an empty orchard with no one in sight. As a sign of civilization after such an uncivilized night, many of the people in the area, though they believed Green had murdered Luella, thought the law should have been permitted to take its course.

Except for what was most likely endless grief for those who loved her, Luella's story might have ended with Amer's death. But there would be more.

Authorities and reporters tried to locate Samuel Payne in Fort Worth, but they were too late. He had left town, said Mrs. Orr, a neigh-

Amer Green hangs from a walnut tree in Walnut Grove near Delphi. Lynched by an angry mob who was convinced he had murdered his sweetheart, Luella Mabbitt, Green may have been innocent and definitely deserved a fair trial. His ghost is said to haunt the grove, forcing a school to close its doors in the early 1900s because teachers and students alike reported seeing his ghost roaming the grounds. Photo courtesy of Jane Simon Ammeson.

bor who had lived next door to the couple. According to author Robert Wilheim in *The Strange Disappearance of Luella Mabbitt,* Mrs. Orr told investigators that Payne's wife said her maiden name was something like Merritt. A pretty woman in her early twenties, she and Payne had been married in Indiana and had moved to Texas from Indianapolis.

As for William Walker, he had been imprisoned in another section of the jail on the night when the mob attacked the jail, but a deputy sheriff hurriedly secreted him in the cupola of the jail residence. Otherwise his fate might have mirrored that of Green's. Instead, he was eventually released.

A Ride and a Rope

Amer Green and a Gang of Hoosiers Take Part in a Lynching Bee

---

A Brother of the Dead Man Says His Supposed Victim Is Alive in Texas

St. Paul Daily Globe (MN), **Sunday, October 23, 1887**

A News special from Peru, Indiana, says Bill Green, brother of Amer, who is in jail in this city, is in abject terror, fearing the fate his brother met last night. There are rumors of lynching but without foundation. He reiterates the statement that Miss Mabbitt is alive in Texas.

GREEN LYNCHING

A Spirited Controversy

Between Governor Gray and Sheriff Van Gundy as to Their Respective Effective Duties

Indianapolis News, **Tuesday, October 25, 1887**

On last Saturday Governor Gray wrote a letter to Sheriff Van Gundy of Carroll County, censuring him for not taking precautionary measures to prevent the hanging of Amer Green by a mob.

STARTLING REVELATIONS IN THE MABBITT CASE

Daily Evening Bulletin (Maysville, KY), July 22, 1887

Logansport, Ind—A new complication has been added to the mysterious case of Luella Mabbitt, who is supposed to have been murdered by Amer Green, who was recently captured and brought to this city. Today the discovery was made by a visit to the vault in Spring Vale cemetery that the head is missing from the body of Miss Mabbitt. Two months ago, William Mabbitt, father of the dead girl, gave a Lafayette dentist permission to take a cast of her head. Mr. Mabbitt now professes ignorance as to the whereabouts of the severed head.

At a meeting at the State Dental Association several weeks ago, the Lafayette dentist displayed a jawbone which he said was taken from the head of Miss Mabbitt. The association decided that the teeth were those of a person fully fifty years of age and further that the person was not a woman but a man. Inasmuch as the remains were identified by the teeth as those of Luella Mabbitt, this assertion proves to be a singular puzzle. The excitement over the capture of the Green brothers remains unabated.

IS LUELLA MABBITT ALIVE?

A Strange Woman Causes Intense Excitement at Delphi, Ind.

Democrat and Chronicle (Rochester, NY), Tuesday, October 25, 1887

The *Journal*'s Delphi correspondent reports that the town is intensely excited over a report that Luella Mabbitt, whose supposed murderer Amer Green was lynched on Saturday morning, had arrived there. Careful inquiry revealed the following:

On Saturday night a young woman, heavily veiled, alighted from an east bound Wabash train, and going up to the baggage room, asked if her trunk had arrived, stating that she had checked it when she took the train at Fort Worth, Texas.

A drawing of Minnie Mabbitt at the time of her trial. Newspapers.com.

The trunk had not arrived and she left the station and has not since been seen. The people and their neighbors deny that any woman answering her description has been seen by anyone in their vicinity with in the last three days and a search of the town failed to reveal anyone.

The trunk arrived a few hours after her disappearance. It is heavily roped and securely locked and there are scores of people who would pay almost any sum could they lift the lid and ascertain its contents. The arrival of this woman and her trunk have set rumors of all kinds afloat and the town is full of people anxiously awaiting developments.

Over the years, others would claim they'd seen and/or spoken to Luella and rumors abounded. Some believed she'd moved to Mexico and married. Others had her in New York. But wherever she was alive and living remains unanswered. When Luella Mabbitt disappeared from Carroll County, she never officially came back.

And then, three years later, Luella's younger sister Minnie May and her two brothers, Oris and Mont, were arrested for the murder of Minnie's newly born infant.

KILLED THEIR SISTER'S BABY

The Mabbitt Children at Indianapolis
Appear to Be a Bad Lot

Daily Tobacco Leaf-Chronicle (Clarksville, TN),
Thursday, December 4, 1890

Indianapolis—Minnie May Mabbitt, the "Mrs. Jones" whose baby was found murdered in Eagle Creek, has confessed. She admits that she is the unmarried sister of Mont and Oris Mabbitt. Charles Spilter, an attendant in the Cleveland insane asylum, she says is the father of her child.

Pregnant at seventeen, Minnie May turned to her brothers, Oris and Mont, to help her as the father of her baby wanted nothing to do with her. Checking into Little's Hotel in Indianapolis under the name of Mrs. Minnie Jones, she gave birth to a little girl who was named Merle. Her brothers gave out the story that she had hired them to protect and take care of her during this time.

What happened next depends on who tells the story, but ultimately Marshall Joseph F. Jenkins of West Indianapolis, acting on a tip from a young man named Hunt, found the body of the baby in Eagle Creek attached to a heavy boot containing a buggy weight.

On the stand, Coroner Manker testified to the results of the postmortem examination. Describing the position of the baby's body, he surmised she'd died from strangulation as no water was found in her lungs.

Continuing his testimony, Manker said the body was in a good state of preservation even though it might have been in the water for several days.

Patrolman Thrust, who arrested Mont, identified the weight found in the bootleg as coming from the livery stable where Minnie's brother worked. There was also evidence that Mont took one of the buggies from Ward's stable on the night Minnie left the Little Hotel.

On the same night the crime was committed, Minnie and Oris were driven to the Massachusetts Avenue depot where she took a train to Flora, where the family now lived.

Days later, when the body was found, two women from Little's Hotel were able to identify her as Merle and the mother as Mrs. Jones. Oris and Mont were arrested. Remaining silent about what had happened, police first feared that Mrs. Jones was dead as well, and under orders of Coroner Manker, they dragged Eagle Creek but no body was discovered. Later a sergeant named Laporte received information that the woman known as Mrs. Jones was actually Minnie Mabbitt and the sister of the men under arrest. He telegraphed to Flora and soon received a reply that Minnie was there and had admitted to being the mother of the child born at Little's Hotel.

Procuring a warrant for her arrest on a charge of murder, on the evening of December 1, the sergeant started after her, accompanied by an *Indianapolis News* reporter. It was late at night when they reached Flora, still half the town was at the depot seemingly awaiting them. But Minnie wasn't among the crowd. Earlier in the day, she had walked out of town.

"Hiring a team of horses, the officer and the reporter started after her," the newspaperman wrote about the experience. "It was a bright moonlight night but very cold, so cold that the occupants of the carriage frequently had to alight and run around the road behind the vehicle to keep from freezing."

Minnie was finally found at the home of her sister, Mrs. William Stone, some miles distant from Flora. Taken back to town, she was locked up overnight, and the following morning was taken to jail in Indianapolis.

Young Minnie must have been a heartbreaker because when it came time to testify on the stand, both the sergeant and the reporter displayed a devoted tenderness and desire to protect her.

MINNIE ON THE STAND

Indianapolis News, **Wednesday, February 25, 1891**

Detailing her arrest and how he treated her, Laporte said he "told her that she need not make any statements that would incriminate herself, and that the Coroner could not force her to tell him anything."

Laporte, advising Minnie to see an attorney before meeting with Manker, sent an officer to bring back the lawyer representing her brothers.

"While testifying Laporte's eyes filled with tears."

The reporter who had accompanied Laporte also testified, as did one other officer, that he told Minnie not to make any statements until seeing Manker.

A SISTER'S BABE: WEIGHTED AND CAST TO DEATH

Minnie May Mabbitt's Infant Consigned to the Waters,
Her Brothers Aiding Her in the Ghastly Child Murder

———

Sorrows Which Follow an Unfortunate Indiana Family

———

The Girl a Sister of the Murdered Lou Mabbitt,
Whose Betrayer Was Lynched by an Infuriated Mob, One of the
Present Prisoners Putting the Rope about His Neck

———

Statement of the Murderess Detailing the Horrible Affair Claims to
Have Been Ruined by a Cleveland Asylum Attendant

———

The Mystery of the Tragedy of Eagle Creek—
All the Parties under Arrest in Indianapolis

Cincinnati Enquirer, **Wednesday, December 3, 1890**

The mystery surrounding the murder of Little Merle, infant child of Minnie May Mabbitt alias Minnie Jones, has been practically cleared up and by the confession wrung from the woman this afternoon Mont and Oris Mabbitt, brothers of the woman, planned and executed the deed.

Driving out toward Eagle Creek with her brothers, Minnie believed her child would be taken to an orphanage or left on a doorstep. Mont took Merle from her, wrapping the babe in a blouse and descended from the carriage. Oris and Minnie drove off and then returned to find Mont waiting without Merle. The party then returned to the city.

"No one told me the baby was dead," Minnie told the coroner. "But I knew it was."

Claiming that Mont never even hinted to her that he intended killing her baby nor that she wanted her killed, she said her brothers had overruled leaving Merle at an orphanage because they were fearful her secret wouldn't be kept for long and she would be ruined.

THE PROBABLE DEFENSE

Logansport Pharos-Tribune, **Friday, December 5, 1890**

> The defense will attempt to show that the child was accidentally smothered at the hotel and that the girl and her brothers, fearing they would be suspected of murder, took it to Eagle Creek to hide it. There is a good deal of sympathy for the girl as she is but 17 years of age and believed to have been under the influence of her brothers when she consented to the crime.

MINNIE MABBITT ACQUITTED
OF THE CHARGE OF MURDER

AFTER BEING OUT TWO HOURS THE JURY
RETURNED A VERDICT OF NOT GUILTY

Logansport Pharos-Tribune, **Monday, March 2, 1891**

> The jury in the case of the state versus Minnie Mabbitt, charged with the murder of her illegitimate child, retired at 7 o'clock

Saturday evening and a few minutes past 8, returned with a verdict of not guilty. Four ballots were taken. On the first ballot ten favored acquittal and two convictions. On the second and third ballots only one favored conviction. The fourth and last ballot was unanimous for acquittal.

When the verdict was read the approbation of the spectators gave vent in applause. Minnie's tears could not conceal her joy and she and her parents were almost overcome by the glad news. It was an affecting scene.

THE MABBITT TRIAL

Testimony in the Child Killing Case—Mont Mabbitt Acquitted

Indianapolis Journal, Tuesday, June 9, 1891

The trial of Mont Mabbitt at Lebanon is attracting as much attention to that town as the trial of Minnie Mabbitt in Indianapolis. The old-fashioned courtroom was crowded and the usual row of morbidly curious women was in place when the evidence began. Minnie Mabbitt, looking spruce in a new blue silk dress, sat by the side of her brother, tears occasionally flowing down her cheeks. Her mother, with shoulders stooped and head bowed, kept her gaze on the floor during the entire proceedings.

Many of the Indianapolis witnesses did not appear and attachments will be served upon them today. The absence of these witnesses delayed the trial and the court was compelled to adjourn early in the afternoon. The trial is before Judge Stephen Neal, with Messrs. Pollard and Ralston for the defense and Messrs. New and Abbott for the prosecution. The statement made yesterday that Oris Mabbitt would turn state's evidence is erroneous. This report arose from the fact that he has been summoned as a witness for the state and will be taken to Lebanon today.

Great crowds attended the next court session with newspapers noted that many were women. [*Author's note:* I ran across many newspapers that bemoaned the fact that women, instead of being home with their own children and taking care of their husbands, were attending murder trials, particularly those of women in precarious situations such as Minnie's].

Oris testified that the three never were intent on murdering the baby. Instead they all agreed to leave it at the doorsteps of some farmer's home and that Mont was to perfect the arrangements.

The parents of the Mabbitt boys took the stand and related the misfortune and troubles that had befallen them over the last few years. As they talked about the murder of their daughter Luella, reporters noted that "much sympathy was excited."

The jury Saturday morning brought in verdict of acquittal.

Last of the Mabbitt Cases

Oris Mabbitt was released from custody yesterday by Judge Cox, who sustained a motion by Prosecuting Attorney Holtzman to nullify the indictment against him for infanticide. Mabbitt did not seem to realize at first what the Judge said to him, but on the latter repeating his order for release the prisoner left the courtroom with his brother Montezuma.

WHAT FOLLOWED

The Ghost of Green

Plymouth Republican, Thursday, July 4, 1901

Jesse Martin, trustee of Jackson Township, is receiving sealed bids for the erection of a school building on the Margarat Knettle farm, to take the place of the Walnut Grove school-house, recently abandoned because of a superstitious belief that Amer Green's ghost was haunting that locality. Some years ago Green was hanged by a mob to a walnut tree near the school-house for the murder of Luella Mabbitt. At numerous times the pupil reported that Green's ghost had been stalking in that vicinity and the school began to dwindle in attendance until only two pupils were left.

Even the teachers at the school told of seeing Amer Green, and the walnut tree, from which he was hanged, never sprouted leaves again.

In 1907, J. B. Stanley, who then was the sheriff, traveled the countryside preaching about the importance of the temperance movement and giving lectures titled "Life, Crimes and Captures of Bill and Amer Green." There's a slight nagging feeling when reading about Stanley that comes from remembering the calm and precise words of Amer Green spoken rationally even as he stood before the angry mob who were intent on killing him. "Buck Stanley will tell you that," he had said about how the then deputy sheriff didn't give him time to produce Luella or talk to his lawyer before bringing him back her. And the "absurd" tale of Luella's hair being found in a trunk was also from Stanley, Amer said. A question arises. Stanley was obviously a good lawman as he was able to track Green and his brother down some two thousand miles away. He was a man whose zeal for abstinence sent him on an evangelical mission to make the world a better place. Did this preclude him from seeing that Amer might actually be an innocent man?

When word came that Governor Matthew was considering pardoning William Green, fifteen years after beginning his life sentence for murder, there was gleeful talk of lynching him. He and Amer were described in a news account as "toughs of the first order."

ANTI-LYNCHING BILL KILLED IN INDIANA

Chicago Tribune, Sunday, January 29, 1899

Lynching remained prevalent in Indiana until 1901, though previously some steps were taken to try to stop it. But with the election in 1897 of Governor James Atwell Mount, a member of the White Caps (groups, mainly in southern Indiana, who lynched people they didn't like, thought guilty of crimes, or just because . . .), the legislation was rescinded.

The antilynching bill, passed by both branches of the Indiana legislature, was sent to the governor for his signature March 7, 1898. It provides that the office of any sheriff from whom a prisoner is taken and lynched shall be considered vacated. The deposed sheriff, however, shall have ten days to present his case to the governor, and the governor has the authority to reinstate an officer when it is proved beyond a doubt that the lynching was through no negligence of his. The law cannot prove sufficiently effective for obvious reasons.

ANTI-LYNCHING BILL PASSED IN INDIANA

Cleveland Gazette, **Saturday, March 16, 1901**

After his death in 1901, his successor Winfield Durbin got a law passed and put force behind the written words. He dismissed law enforcement officials not supportive of the antilynching law, set up patrols of militia in areas where they thought there might be a lynching and investigated local governments that were lax on keeping the White Caps and similar groups at bay. When a policeman was killed in Evansville in 1903, the sheriff sent word to the governor's office of his fear that the suspect would be lynched. The militia arrived and stood between the jail and the crowd. Someone in the crowd took a shot at the militia who responded back by shooting into the crowd, killing one, and injuring eleven. This hard lesson seemed to work. There wasn't another lynching in Indiana for thirty years when two men from Marion were lynched despite the pleas of Katharine "Flossie" Bailey, the wife of a doctor who was president of the Indiana National Association for the Advancement of Colored People, for local authorities to protect them. She worked with the Indiana Assembly to pass stricter antilynching laws and also advocated for one on the federal level.

A GIRL ACCIDENTALLY HANGED

Faint and Fall and Her Neck Caught in Noose

Indianapolis News, **Friday, May 23, 1890**

[Special to the *Indianapolis News.*] Flora, Ind., May 23.—Miss Carrie Mabbitt, the sixteen-year-old daughter of Martin Mabbitt, met death in a peculiar manner Saturday at her father's home, six miles east of this place. The girl had gone to the barn to look after some chickens, and a few' minutes afterward she was found dead by her brother, with her head fastened in a halter, which had been hanging on a beam. It is supposed that she had fainted, and, falling with the halter around her neck, was strangled to death accidentally. Miss Mabbitt was a cousin of Luella Mabbitt, for whose supposed murder Amer Green was lynched by a mob near this place ten years ago.

INDIANA IDEA OF "HISTORIC"

Logansport Pharos-Tribune, **Monday, November 11, 1898**

Friday night during a heavy wind, Carroll County's historic walnut tree was blown down. It was the tree upon which Amer Green, the murderer of Luella Mabbitt, was hanged by a mob ten years ago.

Luella—The Walking Dead?

In February 1916, Luella's sister Ella, who had positively identified the corpse three decades earlier, voiced her doubts about whether Amer Green had really murdered her sister, telling a Logansport newspaper:

For all I know, my sister may have not been murdered and may be living today. One night the home folks were awakened by the quarreling voices of Amer Green and my sister down the stairs. Green was demanding the return of some presents which he had given and Luella was remonstrating. She had been called out of bed and was attired only in pair of house slippers and a kimono. Suddenly the voices were quieted and we went back to sleep. The next morning Luella was missing and no trace of her was ever found except the torn kimono. A body found later in the creek was not identified.

CARROLL COUNTY MAN SAYS WOMAN TOLD HIM SHE WAS LUELLA MABBITT

Miss Mabbitt Was Supposed to Have Been Murdered 30 Years Ago by Amer Green

Logansport Pharos-Tribune, **Tuesday, February 22, 1916**

A week ago yesterday Hezekiah Shanks of Camden was in Logansport and declares he was at the Pennsylvania station when a woman approached him and addressing him his full name, said she was glad to see him.

"That's my name," said Shanks, "but you have the best of me. I don't know you."

"You ought to," replied the woman. "Don't you remember Luella Mabbitt?"

"Yes, but that was 30 years ago and I might not know her now," said Shank.

"Well, I am Luella Mabbitt," continued the stranger. "And now I am on my way to New York where I live."

"At this juncture in the conversation, says Shanks, a train approach and as it did so, the woman replied, "This is my train," and left him without another word.

Shanks' story was told in Camden when he returned home and number of inquiries from people residing in the neighborhood of Camden and Flora have reached the *Journal-Tribune.*

When asked about the report last night, Shanks repeated his odd story of the accidental meeting. He says he did not identify the woman who accosted him as bearing any resemblance to Luella Mabbitt. Sheriff Stanley, who has the most intimate knowledge of the Mabbitt case, declares there is no possibility that the woman who Shanks says accosted him, could be Luella Mabbitt.

Old residents of the county will recall he tragedy in which Luella Mabbitt was supposed to have been murdered by Amer Green and for which alleged crime he paid the penalty at the hands of a mob which took him from the Delphi jail after his capture.

Several years after his alleged crime he was apprehended in a remote corner of Texas by J.B. Stanley, now sheriff of the county.

Author's note: Is it just coincidence that Ella made her statement in the same month and year that Shanks ran into a woman claiming to be Luella as she was about to board a train from Logansport to New York?

Minnie—We Hope She Found Happiness

On February 18, 1899, Minnie Mabbitt, who was born on April 17, 1864, and tried for murder in 1890, married Amos Shanks in Wheeling, Indiana. Minnie died on April 30, 1929, in Carroll County, Indiana, at the age of sixty-five. She is buried at Maple Lawn Cemetery as is her husband, Amos, who was born February 17, 1858, in Cass County, Indiana, and died on November 19, 1943, in Flora.

3

JANE DORSEY AND THE POISON POWDERS

LINKS IN THE CHAIN WHICH TIGHTEN
A MODERN BORGIA IN ITS COILS

Indianapolis Sensational Murder Case

---

*Mrs. John Dorsey Charged with Poisoning Four Husbands,
Her Mother and Sister and Two Children—
The Adults Had Their Lives Insured*

Waterloo Daily Courier (IA), **Tuesday, July 14, 1891**

Jane Dorsey was fifteen when she married for the first time. By the time she was forty and under suspicion for poisoning eight people, Jane Dorsey's beauty was somewhat faded. But then what could you expect? The task of having to send so many people to their graves would wear anyone out. Added to her stress was that Dorsey had caught the attention of Coroner Manker, who found it odd that both her mother and daughter would die so closely together with such similar symptoms and such nice insurance policies.

The bodies were dug up, their stomach contents were analyzed, and grains of poison were found.

Her life has been one of continual romance with a succession of ghastly climaxes. She was only 15 when she met Daniel Sanley (also spelled Stahey), an honest working man. After their marriage he insured his life for $2000.

He lived but two years, and a year after that she married a fireman on the Jeffersonville, Madison & Indianapolis railroad. He survived but a short time and his widow was united to Albert Conkling, a tinner, and with him moved to Camargo, Douglas County, Illinois where he died. She then returned to Indianapolis and in a short time married Joseph Sterret, a widower with two children and he shortly followed her other husbands to the grave, but not till both of his children had died.

Three months ago she was married to John Dorsey and they now occupy a modest little cottage in the southern part of the city which is the residence portion of hundreds of the working class.

The list of husbands may be incomplete because Jane who was also known as Hannah, was said to have been married to a John Temple (he came after Sanely and before Conking—oh what a busy girl she was).

WAS PROBABLY POISONED

Logansport Pharos-Tribune, **Friday, June 19, 1891**

Coroner Manker reported to Superintendent of Police Colbert that a chemical examination of the stomach of Mrs. Nancy J. Wright, who died May 13, revealed the presence of poison in sufficient quantities to kill. Ten days before Mrs. Wright's mother died under precisely the same circumstances and her body will be exhumed for examination. The coroner has informed Mrs. John Dorsey, sister of Mrs. Wright, that she is suspected of administering the poison, but Mrs. Dorsey denies the charge. Mrs. Wright was insured for $1000 and her mother for $680.

CORONER MANKER MAKING AN INQUIRY

Neighborhood Gossip Busy

Indianapolis News, Thursday, May 14, 1891

A visitor to the house overhead Mrs. Wright complaining to her sister, Ms. Dorsey, that "it was the last powder that is killing me." Mrs. Wright's brother who came from the country to visit was so ill he could not attend his sister's funeral.

DID SHE POISON HER MOTHER?

Indianapolis News, Wednesday, July 8, 1891

Examining the stomach of Mrs. Taylor, mother of Mrs. Nancy Wright, chemist Peter Latz found a quantity of arsenic in it.

When John Dorsey was on his way to get a license to marry Jane Dorsey, he met his brother on the street and told him where he was going. "You might as well go on and order your coffin too," said the brother.

"As God as my judge, and realizing that it is probable that I have but a short time to live, I want to say, Doctor, that I am innocent of any act leading to the death of either my sister or mother as you are," said Jane Dorsey to Coroner Manker. "There is only one thing that I do know that might assist your investigation and that is that my sister frequently threatened to kill herself and my mother, too. She was an extremely high tempered woman, and one occasion when she and mother quarreled I heard her say that she would kill herself and get mother out of the way too. Her little girl, Lizzie, heard her make the same threats and so did my sister-in-law, Mrs. Taylor, though at different times."

"Do you suppose," responded Manker with a dry sense of humor that probably comes about by so many murder investigations, "that your dead sister then carried out her threat by poisoning her mother?"

"Yes, that is my opinion since it is shown that their stomachs contained poisons," was Jane's reply.

How They Died

Married to Jane for two years, Sanley died of sunstroke.

She was married to John Temple for six years and he "went from bronchitis to consumption and died."

Third up was Albert Conklin. Their wedded life lasted three years, and then he died in Illinois of congestion of the brain, Jane said. Next Sterret passed away in the spring of 1890. Jane married Mr. Dorsey in February of the next year.

Manker, who had down his homework, said, "Clippings from the papers at the time show that Conkin worked where was employed the day before his death, and, instead of dying from congestion of the brain, died of a violent stomach trouble."

Under pressure from Manker and fearful of what would happen to her, Dorsey grew more fragile and was described as little more than an invalid.

"When the subject of her trouble is broached her countenance changes quickly, tears fill her eyes and she protests with the more earnest vehemence that she is the victim of circumstances and that she is innocent of crime."

Jane did have her champions—or at least sort of.

THE DORSEY CASE

Mrs. Bennet Taylor Tells Some Things about Her

Indianapolis Sun, Thursday, July 9, 1891

Mrs. Bennett Taylor was married to Jane Dorsey's brother and started off in her interview with the *Sun* describing her sister-in-law "as a very sick woman and scarcely able to stand, and I think the papers all over the country are doing her an injustice."

Upset that many thought Jane had killed people, Bennett said they didn't think she had done so but there was a "but."

"If she is guilty," said Bennett, "she is not to blame for it for then it is a mania and she couldn't help it."

Indianapolis Journal, **Tuesday, July 28, 1891**

> Hannah Dorsey qualified yesterday as administratrix of the estate of Elizabeth Wright. This was done to take care of a small insurance which falls to the infant daughter of Mrs. Wright, whose death in May from poison gave currency to sensational rumors concerning Mrs. Dorsey, a sister of the deceased. The coroner still has the circumstances attending that death under investigation.

And with that, the last article found, sobering as it seems with Jane Dorsey being put in charge of both insurance money and a small child, the rest of her story disappears from our sight.

4

The Death of Susan Beaver

ANOTHER HORRIBLE CRIME!
OUR COMMUNITY AGAIN STARTLED!
DEATH OF SUSAN BEAVER!

Weekly Republican (Plymouth), **Thursday, February 10, 1870**

Just ten days earlier, Benjamin Richhart had seen Susan Beaver, a slender, blue-eyed, redhead standing at the gate leading to the house in Warsaw, Indiana, she shared with Richhart's niece Lizzie. Beaver, a seamstress, was talking to wealthy banker Amzi Lewis Wheeler, a political powerhouse from nearby Plymouth in Marshall County. On Tuesday, Susan boarded a train to Plymouth. And on a cold morning on the last day of January in 1870 Richhart received a telegram requesting he meet the 10:05 a.m. train from Plymouth as Phillip Allman was arriving with a coffin carrying Susan's remains.

If that wasn't shock enough for the townspeople of Warsaw, the noon train brought another Plymouth resident—Marshall County Sheriff Henry Logan. By then, Susan's body rested at the Richhart home being readied for internment. All that changed when Logan shared his suspicions about how Susan had died with local authorities. Instead a postmortem was conducted; a coroner's inquest was

Plymouth and North Michigan streets looking southeast in downtown Plymouth, Indiana, around the time Susan Beaver lived there. Photo courtesy of the Marshall County Historical Society.

hurriedly convened; and Warsaw Constable Elijah Blackford traveled to Plymouth to bring back the attending physician and the woman in whose house Beaver had died.

Blackford returned on the 9:43 p.m. train accompanied by Dr. J. J. Vinall and a most unwilling Hannah Hopkins.

Testifying in front of the coroner's jury, Vinall said he'd first come to Hopkins's house on the previous Tuesday to treat Beaver who suffered from a complication of diseases.

"I simply inquired into her symptoms," reads his deposition. "At the time she was suffering as she had always suffered at such times, with sick headache, the pain was in the lower part of her bowels, stomach and head, did not make any examination of her person except at the external portion of her bowels."

Vinall prescribed pulsatilla and belladonna, two common homeopathic medicines at the time used to reduce fevers and infections and to quiet a restless patient. He also directed Hopkins to soak Beaver's feet in warm water and place a warm compress over her bowels. This, Vinall believed, would result in the return of her menstrual flow and her health.

But Beaver didn't get better, instead she grew progressively weaker and weaker each passing day. Stopping by frequently, Vinall tried other medicines including podophyllin, an extract from the American mandrake plant, in combination with quinine in two grains every three hours to help with her constipation, and also ipecac (though normally used to induce vomiting, in homeopathy, it's given to stop vomiting). Susan continued to complain of pain and headaches and her pulse rate dropped. When Vinall saw Susan at 7 o'clock on Thursday morning, he found his patient "alarmingly under the influence of morphine."

He asked Mrs. Hopkins where Beaver had gotten the drug, but Hopkins didn't know. She surmised Beaver brought it with her as there was none in the house and no one else had been in the house besides Hopkins and her thirteen-year-old son. Vinall next prescribed croton oil to move her bowls and left other medicines for Hopkins to inject into the dying woman. She also, at the doctor's recommendation, gave her chloroform.

By then, Beaver's speech was thick and unintelligible, she hadn't eaten for a few days and her pulse rate had dropped to 30. Vinall, who must have been somewhat desperate, administered even more medicines in attempt to counter her constipation and to purge the morphine from her system.

Vinall believed that "if her bowels could be moved she might possibly get well."

But by Saturday night he found Beaver in what he described as "a helpless position." Her bowels continued to be blocked, causing, according to Vinall her extreme prostration which in turn caused her vital powers to sink away.

"It was caused by the disarrangement of the entire system," Vinall told the grand jury the day Susan's body was returned to Warsaw.

Knowing she was going to die, Beaver begged Hopkins to send her body to Benjamin Richhart in Warsaw. One can only imagine the pathos, regrets, and pain that comprised Susan's last days.

Shortly before midnight, Vinall left the house to get more chloroform. Unable to rouse the druggist, he went to his office and then returned to Hopkins's home. But it was too late. Susan was dead and Hopkins, as soon as Vinall arrived, went to find Mrs. Devine to help her prepare the body for burial.

As he sat with the corpse, Vinall said he thought about how during the length of Beaver's last illness, there hadn't been even one visitor at all. It had been just him, Hopkins, and her boy. That was his story, but as authorities would soon learn, he was lying.

Vinall measured Susan's body and set out to see the undertaker, Phillip Allman, giving him her measurements so he could make the coffin that would carry her back to Warsaw.

When he returned, he asked Hopkins for Beaver's pocketbook so he could pay for the $18 coffin he'd ordered. Looking through it, he noted the pocketbook contained a few receipts, several letters, and $36.50.

No one else was at the house the whole time, Vinall repeated to the coroner's jury, and her death, he said, was the result of the large dose of morphine she'd taken, which caused a fatal case of constipation. He had noticed, Vinall responded in answer to a question, "nothing the matter with her in the family way during the entire time."

When it came time for Hopkins to testify, she was at first evasive, but under intense questioning she became talkative and her tale of Susan Beaver's last days was mesmerizing and tragically sad.

Beaver had lived in Plymouth for a while, first with the Allman family and then with Mrs. Babcock who was a milliner. She'd also worked for Amzi Wheeler. Hopkins had known Beaver for the last three years and the younger woman had frequently stopped by to visit.

Though Vinall testified repeatedly that no one else came to the home, Hopkins told a different story. Amzi Wheeler arrived at her door on Monday, January 24, and asked her to take in a woman needing help. This wasn't a first time arrangement between Wheeler and Hopkins. Authorities quickly learned that Wheeler, Vinall, and Hopkins as well as her sister, Mrs. Force, aided young women whose menses had stopped because of an age-old reason—pregnancy. But all that would be discovered after the inquest.

Wheeler promising to pay her "liberally," Hopkins agreed, and the following day Susan came to her home. Hopkins testified that the lamps had been lit for about half an hour (an interesting way of marking time) when Wheeler arrived. Wheeler, Susan, and Hopkins sat for a while before Wheeler and Susan went to Susan's bedroom with Susan closing the door behind them. Maybe the walls were very thin or maybe Hopkins lingered near the closed door, but she was able to hear snatches of the conversation between the two.

"I told you I would not leave you," she heard Wheeler say to which Susan replied, "yes, you did."

Wheeler stayed late according to Hopkins, returning the next day. Vinall soon arrived as well. The three talked a while and then Vinall gave her medicine and used instruments on her, resulting in the delivery of a child.

Asked to get rid of the baby's body, Hopkins refused. Vinall "wrapped it in a cloth at first and then paper and laid it away, at Susan's request, in the box she had brought with her."

The baby, Susan told Hopkins, was Mr. Wheeler's child, and she asked her to go downtown to tell him that she'd had a boy.

But Wheeler didn't care about the baby; instead he asked Hopkins if Susan was doing well. Later the anti-Wheeler newspapers would accuse the banker of being heartless, and so, it seems, he was about his dead boy. But to give him a little credit, he was anxious about Susan's health.

Susan may have wanted to bury her child in the box she had brought along, but, according to Hopkins, in a somewhat contradictory recounting of the event, Vinall took the body, put it in his pocket, and left.

At first Susan appeared to be recovering nicely, but then began to complain of pain and grew listless. Alarmed, Wheeler instructed Hopkins to take good care of his mistress and give her whatever she wanted, saying in front of the sick woman that he would pay Hopkins quite well for her care. He handed her $5, a sum that Hopkins seemed to think was quite generous.

When he came to visit again, Susan was worse, and Wheeler became so worried about her condition, he gave Hopkins $2 more and asked her to go find Vinall. Wheeler stayed with Susan as she ran her errand and returned with Vinall, who after examining Susan, said she was growing more ill. Wheeler then added another $5 to the money he'd already given Hopkin's to help with Susan's care.

Knowing she was dying, Susan, who was still conscious, wistfully told Hopkins she'd been "criminally intimate with Wheeler for the past three years."

"She also said that she wished she had packed her white wrapper as she would have liked to have been buried in it," Hopkins recalled.

When Wheeler arrived on what would be Susan's last night, Saturday, he immediately saw the situation was desperate and again sent for Vinall. Who sat with Susan as she died is murky due to different testimonies, but it appears that only Hopkins remained with her.

The autopsy, performed by Drs. John Leady and Samuel Prince, indicated Susan had died from "puerperal peritonitis (also known as childbirth fever) produced by having an abortion produced on her by some unknown person."

Of course, most people involved in the investigation knew immediately who the unknown person was. Dr. Vinall specialized in treating women with stopped courses. In his signed testimony about the postmortem findings, he said he'd known Susan Beaver for eight years and had treated her for previous conditions that sounded suspiciously similar—the cessation of courses (the newspaper's polite way of saying menstruation) along with a great amount of pain.

"I simply inquired into her symptoms," read his deposition. "At the time she was suffering as she had always suffered at such times, with sick headache, the pain was in the lower part of her bowels, stomach and head, did not make any examination of her person except at the external portion of her bowels."

The grand jury didn't buy his story and shortly after taking the depositions of Hopkins and Vinall, they issued their verdict: "After having heard the evidence and examined the lady we do find that the deceased came to her death by efforts in procuring an abortion by the following persons: John J. Vinall, A.L. Wheeler and Hannah Hopkins, residents of Plymouth, Marshall County, Indiana and which the jury do find caused the immediate death of said Susan Beaver . . . are accessory to said death in the manner as foresaid."

It wasn't the first time Vinall had run into difficulty when treating this type of female "condition" nor the first time that the woman had been a friend of A. L. Wheeler.

The *Warsaw Indianan* ran an anonymous writer's "A Letter from Plymouth," which read:

> The case which I mention as being similar to the Sue Beaver case is that of one Annie Korp, now lying dangerously ill, I am informed at Lakeville, from the effects of an abortion produced upon her by Dr. Vinall. Annie was for nearly a year past, employed as a domestic in the family of Joseph Westervelt, the next door neighbor to A. L. Wheeler. She testified before the Grand Jury that the artful fiend, Wheeler, succeeded after months of effort in seducing her and that after she was known to be enceinte, Wheeler employed the abortionist Vinall to rid her of the child. The abortion, she testifies, was produced at the office of Vinall in the presence of A. L. Wheeler by the use of instruments after which was taken to the house of a widow woman, sister of Mrs. Hannah Hopkins, where she remained until the Sue Beaver case waxed so warm on their hand that they shipped her to Lakeville where she now is.

A separate article in the *Warsaw Indianan* read:

> In the meantime another horrible crime of seduction and ruin by A. L. Wheeler and abortion by D. J. J. Vinall has come to light. This

case is the case of the young and innocent girl, Anna Korp. The young girl is seriously ill and charges her ruin upon Wheeler and abortion upon Dr. Vinall. This case has terribly shocked those among who Wheeler with so much politeness and pretended friendship while at the same time accomplishing his infernal purpose. On last Friday the prosecution took a leading physician of town and visited Anna Korp about eight miles north. The first by the whole of ruin by A. L. Wheeler and abortion by J. J. Vinall. The girl is young and will never be well again. She was at the residence of Mrs. Force, in town, a sister of Mrs. Hopkins, until within a short time. Things becoming too "hot" for Wheeler and Vinall, they forced her to travel to a place eight miles north of town. She says Wheeler was one year in effecting her ruin and did so by promises of money and various blandishments. That he gave her a little money at Mrs. Force's house but after he had affected her ruin he left her shift for herself. She says the operation for an abortion took place in Dr. Vinall's office and that she gave birth to twins.

Many articles viewed Vinall and Wheeler in a melodramatic light as pure evil—the rich, heartless seducer and an incompetent abortionist. As far as Vinall goes, any type of operation before the existence of antibiotics was dangerous. As was birth, where until the early 1900s one out of every three women died during or right after labor, usually of infection. One could argue too, that Wheeler's concern for Beaver was not because he cared about her but that he worried if she was to die, how would they hide the reason for her death from authorities.

Preventing pregnancies in the 1870s was still problematic though there were more options than there had been even decades earlier including the newly improved "rubber goods" (thanks to Charles Goodyear's invention of vulcanization). Besides condoms, vulcanization also led to the creation of intrauterine devices, douching syringes, as well as the wonderfully euphemistic term "womb veils" similar to the twentieth century's diaphragm and cervical caps. Samuel Colgate, who headed a group opposing contraceptives was still willing to advertise that Vaseline cleansed germs (think sperm). Obviously, most of these methods weren't totally effective.

Advertisements promising to restore menstrual flow or provide treatments that were "indispensable to women" were the not-so-secret codes for women wanting to terminate their pregnancy or—in politer parlance—to get their period back.

Vinall used these code words in ads for his services.

J. VINALL, M.D.,

HOMEOPATHIC PHYSICIAN

Particular attention paid of Obstetric Practice and

ACHRONIC DISEASES OF WOMEN

AND

Disease of Children

Office over C. Palmer's Store; corner of Michigan

and LaPorte Streets,

where he can be consulted at all hours.

THE SUSAN BEAVER MURDER CASE

Her Late Residence Broken Into and Her Trunk Rifled!

———————

Further and Complete Particulars

———————

The Testimony in Full as Taken before the Coroner's Inquest!

———————

Disappearance of Mrs. Hannah Hopkins!

———————

Lizzie Richhart Spirted Away!

Warsaw Indianan, Thursday, February 10, 1870

Susan Beaver and Lizzie Richhart shared a room and conducted their dressmaking business in the home of a Dr. Davenport. After her roommate died, Richhart went to visit friends in Ohio and their room was broken into by someone who entered through the window and ransacked Beaver's trunk. The burglar was believed to be

Phillip Allman, the undertaker who had accompanied Beaver's body to Warsaw. His job? To destroy letters sent to Susan Beaver. Unfortunately for Weaver, he left behind the businessman's visiting cards.

Bond for Wheeler was set at $50,000 and denied for Vinall. Wheeler, obviously used to getting what he wanted, demanded that Vinall be granted a bond so he wouldn't be imprisoned before trial. When that was denied, they both, separately it seems, left town. It was said the Vinall fled to Canada leaving his family behind. Mrs. Hopkins disappeared as well, boarding the 2 a.m. train with her son. The two were said to be heading west.

The two men later returned, as did Hopkins who then testified against the two men.

They weren't the only ones to disappear; Lizzie, as we already know, headed to Ohio. A telegram was sent to where she was staying, asking her to return. She did so but then left again soon afterward, supposedly after meeting in the legal offices of Wheeler's attorneys. Rumors suggested she'd been bribed to disappear.

There was other talk of bribery as well. Wheeler, said to be the wealthiest man in Marshall County, certainly had the means to distribute enough money to make witnesses disappear.

When the public learned of A. L. Wheeler's part in Susan Beavers death, there were outcries and accusations about how the difference between their stations in life had influenced the way the case was handled. On February 10, 1870, the *Weekly Republican* of Plymouth published a letter asking what would happen "if some poor laborer or mechanic had even as much as made an insulting proposition to one of wealthy Mr. Wheeler's family?" The same issue reported "the main lawyer of Warsaw, employed for the prosecution, has been brought over to the defense for the sum of $5000."

Interestingly, among the piles of news clippings written about the death of Susan Beaver, most center on—depending which paper you're reading—the absolute vileness of Vinall and Wheeler (the *Plymouth Republican*) or a more nuanced plea to listen to all the facts (the *Plymouth Democrat*). Here it must be noted that the *Plymouth*

Democrat, published and edited by Wheeler's son-in-law Edgar Van-Valkenburgh, was less than impartial.

Yet for all the verbiage, we learn little about Susan Beaver. The *Weekly Republican* said she had "many warm friends here among our best citizens. Many of our most worthy families have employed her and with no suspicions of anything improper on her part. She has been recognized at religions services on Sundays and at other times—but now it seems that while she was industriously laboring to support herself and struggling to lead a life of purity, the 'artful fiend' who has so long held this place in his satanic grasp, was on her pathway dragging her down to a sad and bitter end of agony and death.'"

But there is nothing more than the story of a poor pliable working-class girl led astray by an evil Democrat whose son-in-law owned the rival paper. Where did Susan come from? How old was she? Who were her parents? Besides a description of how she looked (slender, red hair), how she made her living (seamstress), a few accolades to the sweetness of her disposition, her sandy complexion, and how she appeared above reproach as well as the grueling way she died, there are no other clues to her identity. Extensive research by Karin Rettinger, archive manager at the Marshall County Historic Society, found little information about Susan Beaver other than what was reported at the time despite checking numerous newspaper archives and the always helpful genealogical sites such as Ancestry.com and Familysearch.com. Even where she is buried remains unknown. She came from Warsaw to Plymouth, was seduced by Wheeler, and died from the complications of an abortion.

Despite her appalling death, some editors didn't see her as a victim of class, men's passions, grueling poverty, or the lack of adequate birth control. From the *Goshen Democrat,* February 16, 1870, Beaver "established beyond a doubt, that she was and for several years past, has been, but false virtue disguised." Another editor lamented about how common it was for "such girls" selling their virtue to "old covies for $12 apiece" to then seek revenge by having them shot down or prosecuted for damages."

Author's note: We're not sure who these "seduced" women were who had their rich old lovers shot down or prosecuted, as the newspaper's editorial doesn't explain. Nor does the *Goshen Democrat* concede that $12 was a small fortune to a seamstress at a time when even a skilled laborer such as a blacksmith earned less than $1 a day. Pretty dresses, nice dinners, and money might seem a fair trade to a girl who spent sixty hours a week bent over a piece of linen with a needle and thread trying to keep her seams straight as the sun set and she had only the light of an oil lamp.

The story of Susan's fall from grace and resulting abortion followed by her death, all at the hands of one of the most recognizable men in the county, generated an immense amount of interest. The *Indianian* printed six hundred extra copies of their newspaper, all of which sold out by Thursday evening and so ran an additional four hundred half-sheets containing the details of the Susan Beaver case. They also supplied the Marshall County Republican with a thousand extra copies as well.

Imagine the impact of all this on poor Mrs. Wheeler, whose first name was also Susan, and the couple's two grown children.

To give them their due, both Wheeler and Vinall had also experienced tragedy in their lives. Of the nine children born to Vinall and his wife, four had died, which may be why, many surmised, he'd gone into medicine. Wheeler first was married to a Miss Gregory and they had two children, Fannie Belle and Sherman Gregory. He lost all three.

Wheeling also had a major financial setback when younger. Having opened a dry goods store near La Porte, a fire destroyed both the building and the entire contents of his store. Wheeler lost everything and was described as "being several hundred dollars worse off than nothing."

According to his obituary, "he made a clean breast of his financial condition to his friend Sherman of New York who promptly wrote him to rebuild his store, order the goods he wanted and pay for them when he could spare the money from his business. He did so and from that time on he began a successful financial career."

One has to wonder if this Sherman of New York was the reason he and his first wife named their son Sherman.

For those who loved the salacious details (and who doesn't), the *Indianian* reported more about the workings of the Beaver and Wheeler affair. "During the county fair held in that city in October last, A. L. Wheeler visited that place and in company with Sue Beaver and Lizzie Richhart visited the fairgrounds. Wheeler and Sue Beaver left the fair grounds and returned to the residence of the two ladies named. They were seen to enter the house together, closed the door, put down the window blinds and there remain for some time."

The article went on to say that though Beaver "was a poor girl, she had in her possession costly dresses purchased for her, as she said, by a friend of hers at Field, Leiter & Co., Chicago. She was at all times amply supplied with money."

Partisan lines were drawn. Wheeler was a Democrat and a member of the Indiana Constitutional Convention in 1850. Those papers with Democratic sensibilities were more balanced while others, particularly the *Plymouth Republican* were vituperative, even blasting away at VanValkenburgh the editor and publisher of the *Democrat*. But it's also true that abortions were illegal and the abortionist and the woman undergoing the procedure could be jailed.

THE TWO INNOCENTS

The Return in the Night

Vinall Gone to Canada

Wheeler at Home

The $50,000 Bail Accepted

Marshall County Republican, Thursday, March 3, 1870

Dr. J. J. Vinall came back during last week, Monday night and is now at home under bail. He is under bail in the Anna Korp case to the amount of $5000 and in the Sue Beaver case to the amount of $12,000. Mysterious but true.

Wheeler had returned as well and posted his $50,000 bond. That sounds like a hefty sum even now, but in 1870 it was a stupendous amount that, when inflation is taken into consideration, is close to a million dollars. But there was more than bail money to be paid, according to the newspapers or at least the ones not published by Daniel Edgar VanValkenburgh, Wheeler's son-in-law. They were full of stories about bribes being paid to suppress evidence or to get witnesses to make themselves scarce.

But what were bribes compared to Wheeler's fortune? Though Mrs. Hopkins was happy to get her $5 and another supposed bribe of $2,000 to pay off a witness would have seemed a fortune to most people at the time, it was pocket change as far as Wheeler was concerned.

But bribes, generously distributed, must have been successful in this case, because just as quickly as the Beaver case came to the public's attention, garnering immense amount of coverage, it disappeared. It took a lot of searching to discover how the case ended and the results are anticlimactic. Suddenly the intense coverage stopped completely until a short notice appeared in the Thursday, August 25, 1870, edition of the *Weekly Republican:* "Court adjourned last Saturday, with considerable cases left over for next term. The case of Wheeler and Vinall was dismissed."

The following week, the same paper, which had railed against the satanically evil Wheeler, published another small notice: "The case of the state against A. L. Wheeler and J. J. Vinall was dismissed for the want of evidence. This was a foregone conclusion in the public mind in view of all the circumstances."

And so it was done. The following year, a suit against Wheeler and Vinall, filed by Elijah Blackford as administrator of Susan Beaver's estate, asking for $5,000 in damages, was dismissed "because the claim does not set forth facts sufficient to constitute a course of action."

Eighteen months later, the *Plymouth Democrat* had this to say: "During this time, although the public was advised of all the facts as they were revealed, there was no talk of mobbing or hanging anybody and although more than 18 months have passed since the commission of the crime, the parties implicated have never been brought to trial or even indicted."

What Came Next

Susan Wheeler was fifty years old and trying to regain her health at Cleveland Water Cure, Cleveland, Ohio, when she died on Friday, February 28, 1873. According to her obituary, she was the long-suffering wife of A. L. Wheeler, born in Connersville, Indiana, and at the time of her marriage in 1844, was a resident of Wayne County. For the past several years she had been in failing health and in July went to the Cleveland Water Cure to be treated. She became so frail she couldn't return home. She was described as a noble wife and mother being of a modest, retiring disposition, seldom seen in public places.

Author's note: Founded in 1848 by Dr. Thos. T. Seelye, the Cleveland Water Cure Establishment was a combination sanitarium and resort for the treatment of various ailments and diseases through hydrotherapy, specializing in in "treatment of diseases peculiar to females," including ailments related to childbirth.

DIED VINALL—IN THIS CITY YESTERDAY MORNING
AT THREE O'CLOCK, DR. J. J. VINALL, AGED 56 YEARS

Plymouth Republican, Thursday, January 29, 1874

We are informed that he will be buried tomorrow (Friday), at 2 o'clock by the Masonic fraternity. He died of lung disease contracted by exposure, while visiting a patient in Dakota about two months ago. He was brought to this city one month ago, when there was scarcely a hope of his recovery.

Dr. Vinall had been born on May 6, 1818, in Greater Manchester, England, one of at least four children born to Reverend John Juke Vinall and Rachel Thompson. He married Margery Smith in 1840, and they had nine children altogether. The 1850 census shows them living in Cleveland, Ohio, where Vinall worked as a planemaker and Margery was at home with their surviving children, one of whom, Mary, had just died earlier that year at age two. By 1856, Vinall was a practicing physician, and the family left Ohio and moved to Plymouth. The couple's first child, John J. III, born in either 1841 or 1842, had died in infancy, and in 1859 two more, Rachel, sixteen, and Oscar, fourteen, died of typhoid. In 1871, less than a year after the explosive Beaver case, Vinall's wife of thirty-one years died. Vinall is buried at Oakhill Cemetery in Plymouth.

DIED VANVALKENBURGH—AT THE RESIDENCE
OF H. G. THAYER IN PLYMOUTH ON WEDNESDAY,
APRIL 28 OF CONSUMPTION. DANIEL EDGAR
VANVALKENBURGH, AGED 38, FOUR MONTHS,
TWENTY-SEVEN DAYS

Plymouth Democrat, Thursday, April 26, 1877

The editor and publisher of the *Plymouth Democrat,* VanValkenburgh, had studied law and worked briefly as an attorney in Plymouth before becoming a newsman. A rather mysterious ending to his obituary reads, "There were doubtless passages in his life which he would gladly have forgotten and which the grave will cover from the recollections of his friends. He was cared for in his last days by all that loving hands could do, or kind hearts suggest."

There is no mention of his wife, Alice Wheeler VanValkenburgh in the obituary though she was still alive at the time. Whether she was divorced or widowed, Alice remarried again, fifteen years after her first husband's death.

A FORMER HONORED RESIDENT OF CRAWFORDSVILLE
EXPIRES SUDDENLY IN INDIANAPOLIS

Crawfordsville Weekly Journal, **Friday, December 9, 1898**

> B. F. Peirce died suddenly this morning at his home, 1150 north
> Meridian street. His son Edward, and his daughter, Mrs. Lois
> Hughes, who were present, saw their father lurch forward while
> reading his paper. He was dead when the doctor arrived. His
> death is ascribed to apoplexy. Recently Mr. Peirce was strangely
> stricken at Cincinnati but apparently recovered from that at-
> tack. Following this sickness was his resignation from the re-
> ceivership of the Clover Leaf railroad with the announcement
> that he would continue as manager of the I. D. & W. Ry. Since
> coming home he has remained quietly at his residence or hotel.
> No one suspected death was pending. His age was 55 years. He
> was born in Franklin county, but most of his active career was at
> Crawfordsville and Indianapolis.

Successful enough to at one time have his own railroad car,
Peirce married Alice in 1886. According to the newspaper,

> Mr. Peirce did not leave a great deal of property. Besides some
> investments in bonds and stocks, he owned jointly with his sec-
> ond wife, who is now in Persia, the home in north Meridian
> street. He carried about 840,000 in life insurance, payable to
> his children.

DEATH OF AMZI L. WHEELER

Plymouth Republican, **Thursday, May 12, 1887**

> After more than three long years of bodily and mental suffering
> such as few are called upon to endure, Amzi Lewis Wheeler, one
> among the few yet remaining who were here and took part in the
> organization of Marshall County in 1836, passed away on the 9th
> day of May, 1887, at his home in this where he had lived nearly
> 40 years.

On the 28th of March, 1884, and the next day after he had returned from a protracted visit for his health to the Pacific Coast, just as he was leaving the supper table he was stricken with paralysis of the entire right side, completely prostrating him which time he has been totally unable to help himself or to speak so as to make himself understood. His wants, however, were few and those who waited upon him soon learned, as by intuition, what his wishes were and wanting but little, he was easily satisfied.

Mr. Wheeler was born in Seneca County, New York June 13, 1811 and consequently lacked but a few days more than a month of being 76 years old.

After first arriving in Plymouth, Hudson opened a dry goods store. He prospered, establishing a branch of the Indiana State Bank, invested in real estate, made loans and, according to articles at the time, amassed "greater wealth than any other man in Marshall County." Besides business acumen, Wheeler was credited with having nominated and elected to county offices the men of his choice. He also was a member of the convention that framed the state constitution and was three times a member of the State Legislature representing Marshall, Kosciusko and Starke counties in 1839; Marshall and Fulton counties in 1842 and Marshall and Starke in 1855. He was also Register of the land office in Winamac.

Wheeler's daughter, Alice, who had been married to the editor of the *Plymouth Democrat* after her husband's early death from consumption, remarried R. B. F. Pierce. Both she and her brother, E. R. Wheeler, cared for their father during his long illness. A. L. Wheeler is buried in Oak Hill Cemetery in Plymouth.

A. L. Wheeler of Plymouth who was stricken with paralysis over three years ago and who has been almost entirely helpless ever since and unable even to talk as to be understood, except by his nurse, was relieved by death of his suffering on Monday last; an event which he, no doubt, ardently longed for and gladly welcomed. He was about 76 years of age.

Author's note: As for Susan Beaver, she rests somewhere and she may have been mourned, but we don't know any of this as she quickly disappeared from the news. Rettinger, who specializes in historic research and knows much about Marshall County's history says that before my request for information, she knew Amzi Wheeler only as a successful businessman and philanthropist. So, time returned Wheeler to his vaulted status and swept the life of Susan Beaver from history.

5

MISS BRYAN'S LAST CRY

JACKSON'S TRIAL

Pearl Bryan, the Murdered Girl, Was Beheaded While Alive

Some Knowledge of Surgery Possessed by the Murderer—
Mrs. Stanley Identifies Her Sister's Clothing, Etc.—A Dummy in
Pearl's Clothing Removed

News-Herald (Hillsboro, OH), Thursday, April 30, 1896

The midnight moon was full on January 31, 1896, as the cabman ran across meadows and fields of Northern Kentucky. In the distance, the lights of Cincinnati guided him to the Ohio River and safety. Decades earlier many African Americans had followed similar routes as they fled slave owners and sought freedom by going north. Now, George H. Jackson, also an African American, believed he was running for his life as well.

It had started earlier that evening when a man, who Jackson later identified as Alonso Walling, hired him to drive a horse and carriage to Newport. In the cab, shrouded in darkness, sat a man and a woman who Walling said was "sick." Instead of sitting inside with the couple, Walling climbed aboard the driver's seat next to George

Jackson on the Rockaway carriage as they drove toward Newport, a pretty city, just across the river from Cincinnati. But when they reached the city limits, Walling told cabbie to continue driving.

Hearing his female passenger moaning, Jackson tried to get off but Walling, pulling a revolver from his coat pocket, said "You black bastard, if you try to jump out here, I'll send you to hell" and told him to drive on. And so they journeyed further on into the country, through a rolling landscape of fields and farms. Their pace was quick and when they were near Fort Thomas, Walling ordered Jackson to turn on to an abandoned farm road and stop. Getting down, Walling demanded that Jackson turn the carriage around and then wait until they got back. Jackson watched as the two men pulled the woman from the Rockaway and carried her into the darkness. He then heard a woman's screams coming from the direction of where the three had headed. Jumping down from the driver's seat, he hit the carriage lantern in his fall, picked himself up and began to run.

Five days before that fateful drive, Pearl Bryan arrived by train at the Cincinnati Grand Depot.

The daughter of a wealthy stockman, breeder, and farmer, Bryan was from Greencastle, Indiana, a charming college town nestled in a landscape of rolling hills, rivers, and covered bridges. A pretty girl with blonde hair and, according to her mother, a sweet and trusting nature, Bryan had packed her valise and told her family she was going to Indianapolis to visit a friend.

But she'd gone much further than that. Pearl was searching for Scott Jackson, a dental student she had met over a year ago in Greencastle when he'd come to visit his widowed mother, Sarah Jackson. At the time, he and his friend Alonso Walling were students at the Indiana Dental School in Indianapolis about forty miles away.

If Pearl was unassuming and naïve, Jackson, the son of a ship captain who had visited ports around the world, was anything but. To read the clippings, photos, and descriptions of him is to get the impression he was assured, sophisticated, suave as well as cold, cruel, and calculating. But Pearl, much admired and sought after in Greencastle, hadn't figured that part out yet. She had fallen hard for

Downtown Greencastle about the time when Pearl Bryan lived here. Photo courtesy of the Putnam County Historical Society.

Jackson, who with his good looks, blonde hair, and steel-gray eyes, knew how to charm. Now she was carrying his child and wanted to get married before the pregnancy became apparent, which would be ruinous in her small town society. Jackson, for his part, was already seeing someone else and had no thoughts of settling down with a wife and child. Indeed, upon learning Pearl was pregnant, Jackson had sent a packet of abortion powders to William Wood, Pearl's cousin and the man who had introduced the two lovers. But Wood, whose father, Dr. Deloss M. Wood, was the Indiana Presiding Elder of the Methodist Episcopal Church, hadn't given Pearl the powders. She most likely wouldn't have taken them anyway as later events indicate. She wanted her baby and now here Pearl was in Cincinnati, determined that Jackson marry her.

Ironically, Jackson was at the station as well, looking for her while Walling had gone to the city's Union Depot. But somehow

Pearl, whom he called Bird, and Jackson, whom she called Dusty, didn't find each other that night. But it doesn't really matter as their story would most likely not have changed from the course it was on.

Stepping into the terminal, Pearl was carrying a valise and wearing a pretty blue silk dress. On her feet she wore the fine leather and cloth boots with tiny buttons she'd purchased at Lewis & Hayes, a shoe store in her hometown. High quality, the boots were marked in the new-for-America French way showing the last and stock number as well as foot size. A seemingly inconsequential detail, these numbers would ultimately lead the police to Greencastle and reveal the identity of the wearer. But that was in the future and that evening, Pearl hired a cab, directing the driver first to the Ohio College of Dental Surgery on Court Street and Central Avenue where Jackson and his good friend Alonso Walling were students. Unable to find Jackson, she'd had the cabbie drive on, arriving at the Indiana House in downtown Cincinnati where she checked in as Mrs. Maud Stanley, the name of her married sister in Greencastle and sent a message of her arrival to Jackson.

Or at least that's what the cabman who picked Pearl up at the station told police. There was another tale too. A different one, told by Lulu May Hollingsworth, a well-to-do girl with a sordid past. Hollingsworth claimed she and Pearl ran into each other at the station. They'd first met in Terre Haute and then again in Greencastle when May was visiting a friend who attended college there.

Sitting down together in the waiting room, the two began to chat but the subject turned much darker when after a few minutes, Pearl, becoming very emotional, revealed the true reason she was in Cincinnati. "She was in a delicate condition and was on her way to join Scott Jackson, the author of her misfortune," Hollingsworth told reporters, adding that Pearl was considering aborting the unborn child. Supposedly Pearl asked Hollingsworth if she knew of any drugs that would help. "I had had a similar experience and knew what to do. I told her what to get," said Hollingsworth. "The prescription was made up of three different articles."

A cabinet card of Pearl Bryan. Photo courtesy of the Greencastle Public Library.

It was the first of many stories Hollingsworth would tell about meeting Pearl and though the details always changed, all of May's stories ended with Pearl's death.

Though Hollingsworth was a liar, seeking sensation and also to provide Jackson with an alibi, parts of her story were true. Pearl Bryant was about five months' pregnant. But she hadn't come to Cincinnati for an abortion, she could have done that back home with the powders Jackson had sent. No, Pearl was gambling she could finally persuade Jackson to do the right thing by making her his wife.

January 31–February 1

Jackson and Walling frequented a saloon in Cincinnati at Ninth and Central Avenue, owned by Joseph Kugel and located a short distance from where they lived. It was well past midnight when the two entered, carrying a valise, and asked Legner if he'd store it behind the bar until they got back. When Legner was handed the valise he noted, as he would later testify, that something inside "rolled back and forth like a bowling ball."

Later That Morning

Pruning dead limbs from atop an apple tree, seventeen-year-old Johnny Hewling, who worked on the farm of James Locke, looked down and saw a woman's body lying not far away. Her skirt was pulled up and great pools of blood surrounded the body and red splatter stained the bushes, some as high as two feet according to witnesses. Nearby lay a silk kimono, a pair of yellowish-brown kid gloves, black stockings, and a white corset. The victim still wore much of her clothing though, and she still had on her shoes. But there was something missing—her head.

Campbell County Sheriff Jule Plummer and the county coroner were the first to arrive followed shortly by Cincinnati Police Department Detectives Cal Crim and Jack McDermott. It wasn't their jurisdiction, but Crim and McDermott, who would later open a detective agency together, were assigned the job of tracking the type of girls who meet up with the soldiers from nearby Fort Thomas; a monetary exchange that sometimes led to their murders. As word spread, people gathered at the scene and clues were destroyed or removed for souvenirs (there was no yellow crime scene tape then), but investigators were still left with a considerable amount of evidence. When the famed blood hounds arrived, they quickly led the way to Covington waterworks and then refused to budge. Convinced this meant the head was in the vast reservoir that held thirty-five million gallons of water, authorities ordered it drained. The cost was $2,000, two days' worth of time and disappointment. When all the water was gone, there was plenty of debris to pick through but no head.

Evening, February 1

On the evening of February 1, while the city of Cincinnati buzzed with the discovery of the headless corpse, Walling and Jackson walked back into Legner's and asked for their bag. When the tavern keep handed it to them he again noted how the contents rolled about. Fifteen minutes later, the two returned, giving the bag back to Legner. This time it was so light he thought it must be empty. Meanwhile, in the search for Pearl's head, crews dragged the river, dug up sandbars, and drained the aforementioned reservoir without any luck.

Late Afternoon, February 4

If Pearl's identity couldn't be determined by her head, her footwear soon solved the mystery. L. D. Poock, the owner of a shoe store in Newport, immediately recognized the make of the shoe the dead woman wore and also knew that there would be markings that would help identify the owner. Manufactured by Drew, Selby of Portsmouth, Ohio, the numbers 22-11-62458 were inscribed on the inside of the shoe. 22-11 indicated the shoe size and 62458 indicated the stock number.

Looking through their records, Drew, Selby quickly determined the shoes were part of a consignment sent to Lewis & Hayes in Greencastle. Once contacted, the store owners said they'd received a dozen pairs from the Portsmouth-based company and nine of those had been sold. Six of the nine were quickly accounted for and within a few days they were able to account for the other three. Pearl Bryan had bought her pair on November 18, 1895. The victim's overshoes were also purchased there.

Crim traveled to Greencastle, taking with him the victim's clothes. His first stop was at the millinery store owned by Pearl's sister, Mary (Maud Stanley), where he talked to her and their brother Fred. The two shared their fear that they were beginning to believe the headless body was their missing sister. Showing them the bloody clothing, Crim asked if they belonged to Pearl. They answered yes.

Next Crim visited the local telegraph operator who told him about messages exchanged between Jackson, Bryan, and Wood. The latter, when questioned by Crim, revealed that Jackson was the father of Pearl's baby.

Recounting that day in an interview almost forty years later, Crim said he then telegrammed the Cincinnati Police Department with the following terse, to-the-point message: "Arrest Scott Jackson and charge him with murder. Clothes fully identified."

Jackson was arrested the next evening at 10 o'clock as he entered his rooming house, located at 222 West Ninth Street. Four hours later, Walling was taken into custody as well.

There was more evidence. Several blood spots were found on Jackson's shirt and he had a three-inch scratch on his right arm.

Neither Walling nor Jackson had ever bothered to retrieve the valise they'd left at Legner's.

"I have known Scott Jackson and Alonso Walling since December 1895," the tavern keep testified.

They used to come into my place almost every night and would drink.

The last time I saw Scott Jackson was Monday night between nine and ten o'clock after the headless body of a woman was found in Ft. Thomas. He took a glass of beer and gave me the satchel there. He told me not to give it to anybody but himself. I did not open the satchel there. He told me not to give it to anybody but himself.

I did not open the satchel. I kept the satchel until Thursday morning. I read then that Jackson had been arrested and told them I had the satchel Jackson left with me.

After reading about the arrests, the tavern keep took the satchel to the police, telling them about the rolling object that had been inside of it at one time. Tests showed the contents included human hair and blood as well as clay, minerals, and mud matching the soil where Bryan's body was found. Months later, when shown the satchel in the courtroom, Bryan's anguished mother testified that it looked like the one "her daughter took on the trip."

As time went on and Pearl's head still hadn't been found, authorities came to believe Jackson and Walling had thrown it into the blazing furnace at their dental college. Hot enough to destroy the bones and teeth used by students in their studies, the incinerator would have consumed Pearl's head in a matter of minutes.

The police now knew who the victim was but a vital question remained. How did she end up on Locke's farm? By Monday, February 10, police had found two separate witnesses that had seen a cab being driven about 10 o'clock on Friday night and back at the same breakneck pace sometime after 2 a.m. But whose cab was it and who was in it? Despite questioning most of the cabmen in the city they still didn't know the answer until George Jackson turned up at the police station and said he'd driven two men and a woman to Fort Thomas on the night of January 31. Jackson, described by the papers as a "Negro," said he'd been afraid to come forward earlier because the man who hired him threatened to kill him if he told anyone about that night. The police believed his story and had him had tell it again to both the mayor and chief of police. They then asked Jackson to pick out the man among twenty or so prisoners at the jail. Jackson immediately pointed to Walling.

Explaining that they needed to take a sick friend to Newport, Walling had the cabman stop to pick up a man and woman who climbed into the back. Walling opted to sit next to Jackson in the driver's seat and as they approached Newport, pulled out a revolver and told him to drive on. As for the other man, Jackson said he'd seen him twice but only briefly. Once when getting into the cab on a dark street in Cincinnati and then when the two dragged the woman from the carriage.

Jackson's story fit a report that a cab with Bryan and Jackson had driven away from Wallingford's saloon at 7:30 Friday evening on January 31 during a rain shower.

Asked to retrace the journey, a group of carriages left around midnight—the same time as the cabman's first trip only this time there was no moon and the night skies were cloudy and dark. Riding with Jackson were Sheriff Plummer and two detectives. Following them were more carriages and police. Despite the lack of moonlight Jackson followed the unfrequented road with precision, traveling along the Alexandria Turnpike and coming within a hundred yards of the murder scene, but at first he couldn't find the exact spot. Then suddenly he stopped the carriage. Climbing down, he led the way to large flat rock by the roadside.

George Jackson had taken them directly to the murder scene.

On the following Saturday, detectives learned from Chester Muller, a livery stable keeper, that a single seated Rockaway had been hired late afternoon on January 31 and wasn't returned until early Sunday morning, February 1. Muller didn't know who the man was. Carriage, horse and harness, when returned, were covered with mud.

Jackson had told the police that the gray horse he'd drove that night "had a way of lunges and starts and would sometimes take the bit in his mouth and pull the carriage by the reins."

That described his horse, Muller said. As an added plus for the investigators, the Rockaway's carriage light was damaged just like Jackson had said.

Police sent for Jackson who quickly identified both cab and horse.

Jackson's daring escape from the murder scene was another nail—no make that two—in the coffins of the two murderers. If he had waited like Walling ordered him to do, he most likely would have been killed as well. How could Jackson and Walling let him live after all that he had seen?

THE PEARL BRYAN MURDER

A Diamond and Opal Ring Missing

The Story of Laura May Hollingsworth That Pearl Committed Suicide Is Doubted—New Points about Wood and Walling

Wilkes-Barre Times (PA), Thursday, February 11, 1886

It was discovered that a diamond and a pearl ring worn by Pearl Bryan when she went to Cincinnati did not return here with the corpse and the family assert they were taken from the body by the murderer for the same purpose that the head was severed, to destroy the possibility of identification.

The corpse will not be buried for several days in hopes the head will be found.

Another Clue Emerges

Employees of a music publishing company in downtown Cincinnati told Crim they'd seen Bryan walking with Jackson and Alonso on January 30. "When at a spot near the employees who were sitting in a shipping room eating their noonday lunch, the girl was heard to exclaim: 'I am going back to my home and Scott Jackson, you will have to answer to my brother Fred for this.'"

The Defendants

Here is what we know of Scott Jackson. He was twenty-five years old and was five feet six inches tall; his eyes were described by more than one reporter as a cold, glittering blue-gray and his build as wiry and lithe. Born in Maine, he crossed the ocean fourteen times with his father who was a sea captain. After his father died, Jackson lived with his mother, a well-to-do widow, in New York City and New Jersey.

PEARL BRYAN MURDER WAS 113 YEARS AGO

Banner Graphic (Greencastle), **Monday, February 2, 2009**

> Jackson seemed a fine young man. He was considered handsome and was very charming. But beneath the façade of breeding and manners he hid a darker side.

Before coming to Greencastle, Jackson worked in New Jersey as a clerk in the accounts receivable department of the Pennsylvania Railroad. Part of his job was to open the mail each day and add up the checks to be deposited into the railroad's accounts.

His boss cooked up a scheme to steal some of the checks, cash them, and split the money with Jackson. Most of the money was spent carousing at some of the more notorious saloons in Jersey City and a good portion was bet on the horses.

The theft amounted to over $32,000. Audits were ordered and the embezzlement discovered. Charges were filed. The first trial ended in a hung jury over how involved Jackson was in the theft.

In the second trial Jackson exchanged his testimony against his partner to have the charges against him dropped. Following the trial, he left for Indiana where no one knew of his theft.

He enrolled in dental school in Indianapolis and while there, he was fined $10 for consorting with prostitutes and was asked to leave school. He and Walling were also arrested for hitting a man in a fight.

At some point during this time period, Sarah Jackson moved to Greencastle where she lived with her daughter, the wife of Dr. Edwin P. Post, professor of Latin at DePauw University. Jackson, while visiting his mother, became friends with Wood and started going buggy riding with Pearl.

Walling

At five feet nine inches tall, Alonso Walling was taller than Jackson; his hair was dark and his hazel eyes were shaded by thick dark eyebrows. While Jackson seemed to exude poise and charisma and carried himself with a nonchalance and bravado that was appealing to women, Walling was viewed by the press and others who came in contact with him as easily led and under Jackson's sway. Some hypothesized that Walling was only involved in the crime because of Jackson's hold over him. Later, Walling would try to use this as an excuse, saying he had been mesmerized or hypnotized by Jackson.

Jackson's upbringing was one of privilege followed by disgrace and charges of embezzlement; Walling's was much less so. According to the anonymous author of "*The Mysterious Death of Pearl Bryan or: The Headless Horror,*" a surprisingly well-written book despite the sensational title published in the early 1900s, Walling was born on a farm near Mt. Carmel, Indiana. His father died when he was three years old, leaving his mother in moderate circumstances with two other boys, Clint and Charles, to raise. When he was thirteen, Mrs. Walling moved to Greencastle where she kept boarders, and Alonso found work in a glass factory to help support the family. He worked there four years until the factory closed, but by then his mother had been able to save enough money to send him to the Indianapolis Dental College.

"He learned that he worked hard and was one of the foremost in his class," wrote the anonymous author.

> He returned home every evening, and on Saturdays assisted Dr. Sparks, at Greenfield, in his dental parlors. His term expired in March, 1895, when his mother moved to Oxford and made her home with her sister, Mrs. James Faucett. Having very poor health, her only thought was to try and give him a good education.
>
> It was at the Indianapolis Dental College that he first met Jackson and became acquainted with him. By some strange and uncontrollable fatality Walling was thrown with Jackson again

in Cincinnati. Here is his own statement made Wednesday, Feb. 5, 1896, regarding their acquaintance and friendship:

> "I met Jackson in Indianapolis, a little more than a year ago. We attended the Indiana Dental College together. I did not know him intimately there, although we attended the same class. When the school season was over, I had no idea of meeting him again here in Cincinnati."

Mounting evidence against them increased each man's creativity. Walling claimed he'd been hypnotized by Jackson who had a "strange influence" over him. Jackson said he suffered from epilepsy and often had spells lasting for hours. He didn't know what he did during that time and, hence, couldn't be responsible for anything that might have happened.

That defense was used again in 1923 by Harry Diamond who was on trial for the murder of his much older wife, a wealthy widow of a doctor and a pharmacist in her own right. Diamond, a charming and handsome bootlegger and speakeasy operator, told the police he had suffered an epileptic fit at the time his wife was shot four times up close with a Smith & Wesson 38 and beaten with the butt of the gun more than fourteen times around the head. The jury didn't believe Diamond either.

On Tuesday, February 11, 1896, the *Daily Times* (New Brunswick, NJ) dryly pointed out that though Walling and Jackson "have each retained lawyers they cannot be restrained of legal advice from talking."

JACKSON'S WOMEN

Indianapolis Journal, **Tuesday, February 11, 1896**

> Miss Nellie Crane has been mentioned quite frequently in connection with the Bryan murder mystery. While Jackson was in this city attending the Indiana Dental College last winter he and the girl were quite intimate. . . . Crane said yesterday that during the time of her intimacy with Jackson she had never heard

him mention May Hollingsworth nor Miss Bryan. The only woman whom she had ever heard him mention was a school-teacher living in Jersey City, to whom he had been engaged to be married at one time, and with whom he continued to correspond during his residence in this city last winter. He showed her letters he received from the young woman, and upon one occasion told her that he was getting awfully tired of that woman.

"I asked him why he did not marry her," said Miss Crane. "Marry her? If she don't quit bothering me she will get hot foot in it," he retorted angrily, so Miss Crane says.

Some of the letters he received from the young women were threatening, and in one of them she told him that if his conduct towards her did not change she would come to Indianapolis.

"He told me about a good many different women with whom he had trouble. I guess Scott was a great favorite with all the girls. He was always getting in trouble with them, too."

Crane said that Jackson and Walling were almost always together and when asked what kind of a man Walling was, she said he "was a very quiet kind of a fellow and didn't have much to say, not at all like Scott."

Jackson, she said, only mistreated her when he was drinking. "One time he threatened to cut my throat with a razor. We were in Crone's saloon at the time. From there we went to Smith's restaurant. After he drank seltzer and lemon he sobered up some. He said that he had no recollection of having drawn his razor. He was a perfect gentleman when he was sober, but when he was drinking he was the worst man I ever knew."

More Damning Details

The clues (or "clews" as many of the Kentucky papers called them) continued to pile up, creating an impression of a less than perfectly planned murder.

Walling's trousers, splattered with blood and mud stains, were located in his locker at the dental college.

Jackson's coat, discovered in a sewer, had mammalian blood on its lapel, according to Dr. James French, assistant surgeon of the Cincinnati Police Department.

Charles Vickers, complaint clerk of the Cincinnati Police Department, noted that there were blonde hairs in the clots of blood found in Pearl's valise. The wrapper Pearl was wearing on the night of her murder had a hole in it that Dr. Dickore believed was made by the trust of the knife into her neck.

Soil from the crime scene matched the mud found on the clothing of all three. Stupendously idiotic, after going to all that work to remove Pearl's head and dispose of it, Jackson and Walling never got around to destroying the clothes they wore on the night of the murder.

Saloonkeeper Aloysius Stenger testified that Jackson was in the habit of carrying a scalpel around in his pocket.

Dr. H. C. Uhlen, a Cincinnati druggist, testified to selling Jackson cocaine a few days before the finding of the body.

Detective Cal Crim, who had been one of the first at the crime scene, told the court that he had talked to Walling after his arrest. He said Jackson had told him he planned to murder Pearl in early January by luring her to Cincinnati and taking her to a room where he'd poison her, leaving the police and public to believe she'd committed suicide. Jackson later changed his mind and said he would cut her body into bits and dispose of it.

Crim identified Pearl's stockings, gold chain, pocketbook, and other articles found in their rooms. He reported Walling's statement that he wouldn't have warned Pearl of the murder plan even if he had met up with her that first night in the station. He, of course, never warned Pearl during those four days she was in Cincinnati, despite many opportunities to do so.

Time Ticking Away

Four days after the murder, Scott Jackson, still staying at the Palace Hotel, wrote a letter to Will Wood, Pearl's second cousin. "Write a letter home and tell Bird's folks that she has gone away to Chicago and that she has not been at I [Indianapolis]. Tell them she's tired of living at home or anything you want. Get that letter off without a second's delay. Be careful what you write me."

But by the time the letter reached the Greencastle Post Office, Walling and Jackson were in jail as was Wood who had been taken into custody as their accomplice (he was later released). Jackson's instructions were intercepted at the post office. Later, they would be read aloud in the courtroom. Despite their damaging nature Jackson showed no emotion.

Where Was Pearl?

Pearl checked out of the Indiana House on Wednesday, but where she spent the last two nights of her life remain a mystery even though glimpses of her and her murderers were captured here and there.

On Thursday afternoon Walling stopped in a store to ask if there was a skiff for hire to take him across the Ohio River and, when told there wasn't one, he bought a cigar. Outside, the store owner and a woman washing windows saw a blond man and woman waiting for Walling. The owner couldn't see the woman's face as it was windy and she was holding her hat to keep it from blowing away, but he caught sight of her blonde hair.

That evening the three were seen dining at Hayden's Restaurant.

Of course, Lulu May Hollingsworth had a few tales to tell about Pearl's last days.

> Facts that cast a serious doubt upon the story Laura May Hollingsworth who says that Pearl Bryan committed suicide developed here yesterday as a result it is claimed the girl is attempting to shield Jackson and that she did not see Pearl Bryan at Union Station on January 28 daring the time she stopped over here to board a Cincinnati train. Miss Hollingsworth claims she met early about 4 o'clock and that the latter confided the story of her troubles to her and that she gave her a prescription would help her out of her condition.

Lulu was placed under arrest, but a day later was released as authorities believed she had nothing to do with the murder.

MISS BRYAN'S LAST CRY

Heard by a Lady Going Home in Her Carriage

Lulu May Hollingsworth Life

---

*The Indianapolis Girl Released as Her Stories Are False—
Almost a Certainty That Scott Jackson Murdered
the Poor Girl by Beheading Her*

Indiana Democrat (IN, PA), Thursday, February 13, 1896

Not a step of progress has been made toward the solution of the Pearl Bryan tragedy. It has been clearly established that Pearl Bryan confidingly put herself into the hands of her betrayer, Scott Jackson on Monday night, January 27, entreating him to save her and her family from mortification and shame. It was a case of the fly going to the spider for deliverance. Where the too credulous girl stayed on Monday night and Tuesday night, January 27 and 28, is known beyond a doubt. Where she slept Wednesday and Thursday night, January 29 and 30, have remained missing links up to the present writing. On Thursday forenoon and Friday night she was seen. With these exceptions, her whole history from Wednesday, morning when she left the Indiana House up to Saturday morning where her unknown headless body was found remains a blank mystery.

That Fateful Day and Fatal Night

Pat Kinney, watchman at the Grand Central Depot, would later tell the court he saw Walling and Bryan at the depot's waiting room on the afternoon of the murder. He described, and other witnesses corroborated, how Bryan cried bitterly for two to three hours while Walling, they said, was trying to talk her out of some sort of action. He must have succeeded because Pearl never got on a train and instead, at 4:10 p.m., they walked out of the station. If only Pearl had gotten on that train and went home to tell her brother Fred about her predicament.

Though Walling and Jackson both attended classes at the dental school on Thursday, neither did on Friday.

Allen Johnson, described by the newspapers as "a colored porter," said he'd known the two dental students for several months and saw Jackson with a young woman at Dave Wallingford's saloon on the evening of the murder. The girl, who Johnson said was "not of the class that generally visited the saloon," went into the ladies' room where she stayed for about fifteen minutes. During that time, Jackson borrowed $2 from Wallingford, which we doubt he ever got back.

They ate dinner and, according to the Banner Graphic, "Jackson ordered a whiskey for himself and a sarsaparilla for Bryan. In his pocket was a small bottle containing sixteen grams of cocaine dissolved in water. Before returning to the table he emptied the contents of the bottle into Bryan's drink."

Outside, at the George Street entrance to the saloon, Walling was waiting with the hired Rockaway. Pearl and Jackson climbed into the cab and they rode off. Shown the clothes Pearl was wearing when she was found in the field in Kentucky, Johnson identified them as the same as those worn by Jackson's companion.

The defense tried to get Johnson to say he was mistaken about the date, but he stuck to his story. In a sworn statement, Johnson also said that defense attorney Shepherd had offered to pay him not to testify.

Arrogance and Undoing

In one of the more bizarre turns in a case that was already more than odd, the court allowed an interview among Chief Deltech, Scott Jackson, and the saloonkeeper who might have had Pearl's head in his possession for a while.

Jackson said he knew Kuegel and admitted having left the valise in Kuegel's place.

Kuegel identified the valise. Then Jackson was asked about it and said: "Yes, that is Pearl Bryan's valise. She brought it with her. She had her clothes in it."

Deltech put the valise on Jackson's knees. He told Jackson to open the valise and put his hand in it. Jackson hesitated but he opened the valise and put his hand in it.

"What are those stains?"

"They look like bloodstains," Jackson answered.

"Are they bloodstains?" asked Deltech.

"Yes they are," he replied.

"Was Pearl Bryan's head in that valise?" Deltech asked.

"Yes, it must have been, but I am not certain," Jackson answered.

"Did you leave the valise at the saloon?" asked Deltech.

"No, Walling did," answered Jackson.

"What became of her clothes?" asked Deltech.

"I made several trips to the river and disposed of them," Jackson replied.

"What became of the head?" Colonel Deltech asked.

"Was cut up in pieces and then thrown away," the prisoner answered.

The Undertaker's Story

Edward Black, the undertaker who accompanied Pearl's body from Cincinnati to Greencastle, told a graphic story of Jackson and Walling when they were taken by police to view Pearl's body.

The two students stood on either side of the bier, said Black, noting Pearl's sister, Mrs. Stanley, her brother Will Bryan, and several officials were also present. The hope was that seeing the headless corpse and listening to the entreaties of the bereaved family might stir the killers' consciences and they might confess.

"Jackson acted as if completely heartless," said Mr. Black. "He lowered his eyes when brought to the presence of the body. I could not discover one bit of evidence in his manner of any feeling. I thought Walling was a trifle nervous, but both of them were as composed as the others who simply served as witnesses. Jackson would not look the brother of Pearl in the face and he dodged Will's glances all during the proceeding."

Chief Deltech acted as the questioner. The room was as silent as could be and everyone was holding their breath when Mr. Deltech broke the silence by addressing Walling:

"Do you recognize the corpse?"

"I do not."

"Do you know who it is?"

"I believe it is Pearl Bryan."

"What reason have you for this belief?"

"What Jackson told me."

"Jackson, do you recognize this corpse?"

"I do not."

"Do you know that it is the body of Pearl?"

"I have not taken a close and careful look."

"Would you recognize it if you did?"

"I think I would."

"Waling, did you kill this woman?"

"I did not."

"Jackson, did you kill this woman?"

"I did not."

"And do you deny, in the presence of the corpse, that you killed her?"

"I do."

"During the interview," continued Mr. Black. "Walling allowed his eyes to rest quietly on the body in the casket. I have never seen such a quality of nerve as given by these two men."

The two dental students also didn't break when Mrs. Stanley fell to her knees, crying and begging they tell the location of her sister's head. Neither man replied.

Jackson on Trial

Jackson and Walling had separate trials, with Jackson's scheduled first.

One of the first things the jury learned was that the examining doctors believed Pearl had been alive when decapitated. "They

Pearl Bryan is one of the participants in this Arbor Day photo taken in 1891 in Greencastle. Photo courtesy of the Greencastle Public Library.

based their belief on the fact that all the blood was pumped out of her system at the scene and that for this to be possible it would be necessary for the heart to be beating when she was beheaded."

Coroner W. S. Tingley was the second witness the prosecution called to the stand. He described the position of the body when he first arrived at the scene. Situated on a slight rise or terrace of an abandoned roadway, Pearl's feet were on the terrace and the rest of her body below, lying prone on the road.

News-Herald (Hillsboro, OH), April 30, 1896

> She was clothed in combination, underwear, shoes, stockings, tea gown, and dark blue skirt.
>
> The bloody dress, the stained underwear and other ghastly articles were spread in full view before the witness box. Mrs.

Stanley [Pearl's sister] leaned forward, and with wonderful composure considering what she suffered, she identified the blue skirt, the underwear and the green figured dress of Pearl Bryan.

The valise, shoes, hat, etc. of the murdered girl were also described and positively identified by the witness.

Mrs. Stanley testified she knew Scott Jackson from seeing him twice on the streets during the holidays. Jackson was then face to face with the witness.

"This is Scott Jackson," she said.

Mrs. Stanley was not cross-examined by the defense.

Next, eighteen-year-old Joseph E. Peary, a druggist from Greencastle, took the stand, identifying the pocketbook found in Scott Jackson's valise as one he sold to Pearl.

When Mrs. Bryan, Pearl's mother, was examined by the prosecutor, she pointed out Jackson and said he was a frequent visitor to their home. Her daughter, she said, "often went out riding in a buggy with him." She identified the clothing on exhibition as belonging to her daughter.

Testing of Pearl's stomach contents by Dr. W. H. Crane of Cincinnati showed the contents contained about one-and-a-half ounces of cocaine, which he believed entered her body through the mouth. To prove that it was cocaine, he performed a number of corroborating tests. First, he tasted the crystals (now remember these came from the dead woman's stomach) and as they numbed his tongue it indicated it was cocaine. Crane also tried putting a few crystals on the eye of a rabbit, which caused it to become enlarged. He then touched the eye with a hot match. The rabbit didn't flinch nor show any sign of pain. More proof, Dr. Crane explained, as corneas are usually extremely sensitive to the touch.

Weren't They Smarter than This?

Dr. W. D. Litter of Leesborough, Kentucky, a witness for the prosecution, met Scott Jackson about six months before the murder though he didn't know him well. Ten days before Pearl's body was discovered, Litter was passing by the room Walling and Jackson shared when Jackson called him in, asking if one grain of cocaine in a gram of water would have the same effect as the same amount in one-half gram. Jackson thought it would but Walling disagreed.

What did Litter think, the two asked him, to which he replied he thought it would.

The Big Brother

When Fred Bryan—the brother that Pearl had said Jackson would have to answer to—took the stand, he told the crowded courtroom (tickets were issued because so many people wanted to watch the trial), that Scott Jackson frequently called on his sister.

Bryan also described taking his sister's body to the undertaker for embalming and then escorting the remains home to Greencastle where his parents and other family members gathered to view her headless body.

Reading Fred Bryan's testimony, he indeed appears as a man that Jackson, described as cowardly by one source, would have avoided at all costs. He stood stoic as he guided his family through the heinous murder. His parents, elderly at that point, had already lost another daughter a few years before. It's easy to speculate that they must have seen the handsome dental student as a good catch for Pearl, and a sense of betrayal must have added to their grief.

But the most dramatic part of Fred's testimony came when the satchel was brought forth by the prosecution.

Yes, it was his, Fred said, he'd bought it in Indianapolis five years earlier. Drawing a set of keys from his pocket, Bryan selected one and placed it in the lock. Turning the key, the lock clicked into place. Then as the courtroom watched he handed the satchel back to prosecutor Colonel Nelson who entered the key into evidence.

WELDING THE CHAIN

Evidence Connecting Walling with Pearl Bryan's Murder

Testimony of New Witnesses

---

*The Prisoner Seen with the Murdered Girl on the Day
She Met Her Death. Expert Testimony Produced—Coachman
Jackson Story Corroborated—Scott Jackson Weakening*

Evening Bulletin (Maysville, KY), Saturday, June 6, 1896

The most important testimony yet secured in the trial by new witnesses who had not been found when Scott Jackson was tried. Mrs. Elizabeth Ware, keeper of the tollgate near the scene of the murder of Pearl Bryan, testified that about 3 a.m. February 1, a one horse carriage rushed through without paying toll. She heard them coming and tried to get out in time to collect toll. She called after them, but they dashed on, paying no attention to her.

Albert Shrader, the distiller on Licking Pike, testified to seeing the carriage going south on the morning of February 1 at 2 a.m.

Importance is attached to both of these witnesses, as they corroborated the evidence of George H. Jackson, the colored coachman, who testified in the Jackson case to this route being taken when he was driving the rig with Walling on the front seat with him.

Though Jackson and Walling would both later claim that Pearl did have an abortion (and each said the other performed it), an autopsy proved this untrue. Later the two dental students said that a doctor in Northern Kentucky had performed the operation. That was quickly disproved as well when it was discovered the Kentucky doctor was mentally ill and in a sanitarium at the time of the said procedure.

All this begs the question, If Pearl was pregnant when she died, why claim her baby was aborted?

What Were They Thinking?
Questions We Wish We Could Ask

Why didn't Jackson just jilt Pearl and move back East? Sure Fred Bryan would be angry but what really could he do? By the late 1800s, duels were no longer a form of settling differences in America though lynchings still continued.

Or why not marry Pearl? He obviously had spent a lot of time with her during their courtship. She was described as pretty, blonde, charming, and a favorite in Greencastle; she was known for her kindness and wit. And her family was well-to-do. Even if the marriage didn't work out, there was always divorce. Indeed, the divorce rate had risen from 3 percent of the total number of marriages between 1867 and 1879 to 8 percent between the years of 1901 and 1906. That's quite an increase considering that women still couldn't vote in many states, were typically consigned to roles within the home, and had little access to good-paying jobs. Sure, you had to prove abuse, adultery, or abandonment, but it could be faked and often was.

If they were going to carry out such a heartless and despicable act, why not destroy as much evidence as they could? Cutting off Pearl's head certainly delayed her identity being discovered. If Will had received the letter instructing him to write "Bird's" folks in Pearl's handwriting saying she'd left for Chicago, it might have worked. But then again, Pearl had been seen with them out and about in Cincinnati for four days. And she had a telltale wart on her thimble finger. With the amount of press a headless corpse engendered it's hard to believe that somehow her family wouldn't have figured out the girl in the Kentucky field was Pearl. And would Will Wood really have helped them cover up the murder of his second cousin, one he was close to?

Then there were all those damn clues. Why not just toss the valise as well as her head into the fire? Why give it back to the saloonkeeper?

And why bring Lulu May into the mix? With her histrionic nature and inability to tell a straight story, she only made matters worse.

HAT FOUND

Scene of Pearl Bryan's Death Perhaps Located

Gives Kentucky Jurisdiction

Continued Search for the Head Proves Unavailing

An Indianapolis Witness

Miss Hollingsworth Advised the Criminal Use of Drugs

Thinks Death Was Self Inflicted

Courier Journal (Louisville, KY), **Monday, February 10, 1896**

Hollingsworth was quoted in the *Courier Journal* as having brought three types of drugs for Pearl and instructing her to buy another drug after she reached Cincinnati but to be careful of it as it was deadly poison and would kill her if not used correctly. According to Lulu May, Pearl replied, "I will go to Cincinnati and take the stuff and if it kills me I will be near Jackson and he will have to swing for it."

Hollingsworth said she was talking to the press as she wanted to keep Walling and Jackson from being convicted because she thought they were innocent and Pearl had committed suicide. A typical Lulu story is as follows:

> Pearl took the medicine herself. She was in Jackson's room at the time. It had a different effect from what she expected and she grew so bad that Jackson saw she was going to die. He knew that it would never do to have her die in the house so he secured a hack and, assisted by Walling, took her across the river. She may have died on the way or have been dead before they got her out of the room and their object in taking her was to hide the crime. When near St. Thomas, they cut her head off it to avoid identification. See if it don't come out that way.

Lulu May Hollingsworth, who brought to light yesterday as an intimate friend of Pearl Bryan, the girl found murdered at Fort Thomas, late tonight crowned her confessions by finally declaring that she herself had performed a criminal operation on Miss Bryan. Early this evening she confessed that Miss Bryan and Walling had been here on Thursday night before the murder. After continuous work by the detectives she weakened further about 10:30 tonight and told why she believed the victim had died of a criminal operation. Walling and Miss Bryan, she declared, had an appointment with her Thursday evening and she met them upon their arrival from Cincinnati. Walling and the girl spent the night either at the American or Fields hotel. The Hollingsworth woman went there at 4 o'clock Friday morning and met Miss Bryan and they walked down Kentucky Avenue to the Cleveland block. There a room had been engaged but Pearl Bryan refused to go into it. They then sat down on the stairs and then and there, according to her statement, the Hollingsworth woman performed the operation with an instrument brought from Cincinnati by Miss Bryan. After it was over they went to Union Station and the victim was left along at 5:30 o'clock. She told the Hollingsworth woman she would meet Walling there and they would take the train at 6:50 for Cincinnati. May Hollingsworth says she believes she died that same day or evening in Jackson's room in Cincinnati.

The story of Miss Hollingsworth seeing her in Indianapolis on January 28 is exploded by the established fact that she was here on both the 27th and 28th. Two careful postmortem examinations absolutely preclude abortion, natural or attempted, as well as death by poisoning. The universal belief is that the Indianapolis girl is romancing. The knife cuts on the poor girl's hand were made while struggling for life with her murderers and the pool of blood where she lay set at rest the theory she was first killed by anesthetics and then taken out and beheaded.

A Kentucky woman going home in her carriage late Friday night heard a woman's scream followed by silence near Fort Thomas. Men in Covington and Newport, Kentucky remember seeing a vehicle passing at an unusually later hour Friday night driven at great speed. Detectives are working these clues. Not a trace of the head has been found.

Indianapolis special report: After doing more or less talking Lulu May Hollingsworth has made herself notorious by her alleged knowledge of the Pearl Bryan murder, has been released from police headquarters. Police Superintendent Colbert says that he is satisfied that the girl has been lying all the way through and as the Cincinnati police say that they do want her, the Indianapolis police have no further use for her.

HOLLINGSWORTH'S STORY

Indianapolis Journal, **Tuesday, February 11, 1896**

Laura (Lulu) May Hollingsworth, now mentioned in connection with the murder of Pearl Bryan, was formerly a Vincennes girl. Her relatives are among the wealthiest and most respected citizens of that city and the surrounding county. She is a daughter of ex-county treasurer Spencer Hollingsworth, who was found to be a defaulter to the amount of $3,000. He was sentenced to the penitentiary and served his time. Lulu May, or Laura, as she was known here, was inclined to gayety, and had a penchant for forming friendships with strange men on slight acquaintance. On discovering her romantic turn, her guardian sent her to Coates College, at Terre Haute, where she first met Pearl Bryan, the murdered girl. Disliking the restraints of college life, she ran away and created a sensation by her mysterious absence.

In 1893, the *Logansport Pharos-Tribune* reported she'd disappeared from Coates College in Terre Haute apparently to meet a man named Rolla Burwell in Troy, Ohio. Though her father, Spencer Hollingsworth, threatened to go to Troy, Lulu turned up in Indianapolis a week later where authorities found her purchasing a ticket to Cincinnati. She told them she'd run away because the other women at college were taunting her about Spencer's conviction. As her mother was dead and she didn't want to see her father again, Hollingsworth said she was determined to make her own way in life.

LULU

How She Escaped and What Became of Her Clothes

Greencastle Star Press, **Saturday, February 25, 1893**

With those wonderful headlines, we learn that Lulu was not just entangled with one man from Ohio but also with the son of a wealthy druggist from Terre Haute as well as a gentleman from Vincennes.

Persuaded to return to college, she declared to the papers that "she is living an honest life."

Lulu was back in the news six years later.

SWOONS AS DOCTORS WORK TO SAVE LIFE

Lulu May Hollingsworth, of Pearl Bryan Fame, Figures Again

Indianapolis Journal, **Thursday, December 10, 1903**

James Ellis, who attempted to commit suicide early yesterday morning by taking a large quantity of strychnine while in his rooms at 412 East New York Street, is now considered out of danger. Ellis lives at the home of Lulu May Hollingsworth, who attained much fame during the Pearl Bryan trial as being the last girl seen alive with the murdered young woman.

While he was writhing in agony from the effects of the drug Miss Hollingsworth was swooning away in an adjoining room. After Ellis was brought out of danger it required several hours' work for the dispensary physician to bring the young woman out of danger as she seemed on the verge of nervous collapse.

March 20, 1897: A Chance for Redemption
Not Taken

Jackson stood on the gallows, as cool and steady as ever. Onlookers described him "as standing erect and playing the part of an actor." But Walling kept his eyes down as his body trembled. Asked again if he had anything to say, a reporter wrote, "Jackson hesitated fully two moments before he replied. Before he spoke, Walling turned expectantly evidently believing Jackson would speak the words that would save his life, even while he stood on the brink of death. Walling had half turned around and he stood in that position with an appealing expression on his face, while Jackson without looking at him, upturned his eyes and replied, 'I have only this to say, that I am not guilty of the crime for which I am now compelled to pay the penalty of my life.'"

He was as cruel at the end of his life as he had been when he murdered his lover and the mother of his child.

When asked if he had any comments, Walling didn't tell where Pearl's head had gone—an act which would have provided tremendous relief to those who loved her. Instead he responded, "Nothing, only that you are taking the life of an innocent man and I will call upon God to witness the truth of what I say."

When the gallows trapdoors dropped out from beneath their feet, the ropes didn't immediately snap their necks and instead they slowly strangled to death. It was a painful death but nothing compared to the grief and despair they had caused those who knew and loved Pearl Bryan.

AFTERMATH

The Deadly Folding Bed

Phillipsburg Herald (KS), Thursday, March 23, 1899

> Mrs. Bella Yates, a Topeka widow, was shut up in a folding bed the other night. Her stifled cries brought help just in time to save her life. As it is, her spine is injured and her limbs partially paralyzed.

Bella, born in 1850, was Pearl Bryan's older sister. Bella was expected to live but unfortunately her injuries were too severe. And so the Bryans lost another daughter.

For many years, Pearl's five-and-a-half-month-old fetus, stored in a peppermint jar, was on display for a price at A. F. Goetz Pharmacy in Dayton, Kentucky. Its present whereabouts, if it still exists, are unknown.

In November 1899, a young lady requested her gold fillings, put in by Scott Jackson while he was a student at the Indianapolis Dental College, be removed. After the death of Pearl Bryan, her teeth started hurting. Once the gold was removed, the pain vanished as well.

Greencastle grieved, but residents seethed as well. Will Wood left town hurriedly on a Saturday afternoon. "Had he remained here," a reporter wrote, "the result would have been sorry for him."

"It is this way with us," said a citizen to a correspondent for the *Indiana Sentinel* (May 31, 1896), "we are thoroughly aroused over this terrible affair. We have read of dreadful cases, but this is the first time a case of this nature has been brought home to us. We feel that devils have entered here and stolen the life of a young woman who was sinless before they came and who was consequently confiding."

Wood eventually joined the Navy.

A. W. Early, an operator for the Western Union telegraph station in Greencastle, was also a target for the town's anger. Though no one considered him culpable in Pearl's murder, they were outraged that he knew what the three young people—Bryan, Jackson and Wood—were up to and did nothing to stop it.

"There is a belief that it would have been far more noble for Mr. Early to have prevented the first steps and kept Pearl Bryan from leaving home, knowing full well the danger which was attached to such a trip," reported the *Journal*.

Early was removed from his position. His replacement? J. R. Waltz who had been away attending dental college in Indianapolis.

Surviving Artifacts

"What we have is a valise that her killers supposedly put her head in after they murdered her," says Jan Lester, a volunteer at the Campbell County Historical and Genealogical Society.

We don't know if that is really true, as there is no provenance to go with it. We have a pair of handcuffs that were used on one of the killers. We have newspaper articles about the murder, the trial and the subsequent hanging of the two men found guilty of the crime. We have a photo of the scaffold where they were hung which was the last public hanging in Newport and a photo of Pearl's headstone, but she is buried in Indiana.

A WEIRD PICTURE

Indianapolis Journal, **Monday, February 10, 1896**

The cemetery was white with snow when the hearse carrying Pearl's white casket with the word Pearl written on the outside of it. Friends and family followed in two carriages. It was still night and townspeople were asleep so that the cortege was alone as it made its way.

The public vault was open and tenderly the casket was placed therein. The snow, the silence of the night and the solemnity of the occasion all went to make a weird picture.

This morning the sun made an effort to shine forth and its glare was on all the country surrounding when Mr. and Mrs. Bryan, the aged parents, visited the vault to view the body of their murdered child. Undertaker Black removed the casket lid and as he did so, the light of the sun is said to have shone in the gloomy vault. The parents bowed over the open casket and wept, unobserved by others. The ugly gap where the head was severed from the body was protected from gaze by the neck of the dress being drawn together by lace. The body was clothed in the satin when she graduated from high school. Her feet on them satin slippers while the hands were placed naturally by the side of the body. The parents lingered for some time and then withdrew to return to their home which in a fortnight has been transformed from one of happiness to deepest mourning.

Pearl Bryan is buried at Forest Hill Cemetery in Greencastle. Even today, more than a century later, visitors to her grave leave pennies, head side up on top of her tombstone. Since her own head was never found, the hope is these pennies will help her find it on Resurrection Day.

6

ROUGH ON RATS:
HOW NOT TO WIN YOUR MAN

CHARLES KOESTERS TO MARRY: ANNIE WAGNER
REPORTED TO HAVE RETURNED TO GERMANY

Indianapolis Journal, **Tuesday, May 29, 1894**

> Charles G. Koesters, whose family was presumably poisoned a
> year ago, is to be married again. Last night he secured a license
> to marry Mrs. Henry Hoerst, and the ceremony will be per-
> formed today. Mrs. Hoerst is the widowed daughter of Leopold
> Spitznagels, a South Meridian-street saloon keeper. Koesters
> has three children who escaped the fate of the other four mem-
> bers of the family.
>
> Annie Wagner reported to have returned to her home in
> Germany.

Without knowing the history of the people involved, this seemly
innocuous article could easily be overlooked. Few, if any, reading
the *Journal* story today would have even the faintest idea of how
much was summed up in that short, ironic, and understated piece.
It told a much longer and complex story of pain; suffering; the
deaths of a wife, two children, and elderly parents; and the ensuing
notoriety that followed.

ARSENIC IS FOUND

In the Stomach of the Year-Old Koesters Child

The Poison Is Visible under the Microscope

An Investigation Being Made by Dr. Barnes

THE EVIDENCE IS GROWING

And Now Points Strongly to Annie Wagner's Guilt

*The Girl Makes a Statement to the Coroner under Oath,
Which Tallies Well with the Story She First Told*

Indiana State Sentinel, **Wednesday, May 31, 1893**

*The Bodies of the Dead Koesters Are Exhumed and the Stomachs
Removed to Be Subjected to the Test of a Chemical Analysis—
The Finding of the Arsenic in the Stomach of the Babe Makes
Stronger the Chain of Circumstantial Evidence Tightening
about the Wagner Girl—Events of the Day*

THE BODIES EXHUMED

*Chemical Analysis to Be Made of the Stomachs—
Suspicious Indications*

Indiana State Sentinel, **Wednesday, May 31, 1893**

About 6:30 o'clock yesterday morning an unusual scene might
have been witnessed in the German Catholic Cemetery, which is
situated about a mile south of the Belt railroad on the Three Notch
Road. At that hour Constable Cook accompanied by the three "colored" grave diggers, entered the cemetery for the purpose of exhuming the bodies of four members of the Koesters family, all of
whom are supposed to have poisoned by Annie Wagner, the young

German girl who is now a prisoner in the county jail charged with crime.

The men act immediately to work and in a very short time the coffins are taken from the graves and by the time Coroner Beck, accompanied by Drs. Erastus Eisenbeiss, Carey, Young, Ryer and Spin, Per Obler, Undertaker Fitzhugh, Charles and Frank Koesters and George Borst, the druggist who sold the box of Rough on Rats to Anna Wagner on Monday before the crime was discovered, arrived, they all had been removed and were resting in the shadow of the little chapel.

The first coffin opened was that of the babe which was found dead in bed on the morning of January 6. The body was much decomposed and it was with the utmost difficulty that the autopsy was held. The stomach and its contents were removed and placed in a jar brought along for that purpose. The body of Mary M.A. Koesters was next examined. She died February 27. It was found to be in a terrible condition, even worse than that of the babe. A peculiar thing was noticed about this body. While it was in a terribly decomposed condition the stomach was found to be in the best state of preservation. This, the physicians state, is evidence to show the stomach may have contained arsenic.

Undertaker Fitzhugh, who has made a careful study of the action of poison on the human body, said that the stomachs and intestines had that peculiar metallic luster which is seldom seen except in cases of arsenical poison.

MORE ARSENIC FOUND

Indianapolis News, Thursday, June 1, 1893

Dr. Eisenbeiss is making the analysis of the stomachs of the dead members of the Koesters family, says that he has discovered arsenic in the stomach of Frank M. Koesters, which has been in his charge since Tuesday morning. This makes three of the family in whose stomachs arsenic has been found in sufficient quantities to cause death. Two more of the stomachs remain to be examined.

It was reported by the *Chicago Daily Tribune* on Friday, December 15, 1893, that Eisenbeiss, noting that the minimum fatal dose of arsenic for adults is 2 grains, found 7.22 grains. Someone, it seems, wanted to make sure Clara would be dead.

A MODERN BORGIA

The Death of Five Persons in One Family Is Laid at the Door of Young Annie Wagner, Who Is a Domestic Employed by the Family

LOVE CAUSED THE CRIME

A Case with No Parallel in the History of the City

The Coroner and the Police Officers Investigate and Secure Evidence against Annie Wagner

---

The Last Death, Which Occurred Tuesday, Aroused Mr. Koesters's Suspicions and He Came to the Conclusion That Five Members of His Family Had Been Poisoned—Startling Evidence Soon Discovered against the Domestic—Mr. Koesters Thinks the Girl Wanted to Get Everybody Out of the Way So She Could Marry Him—One of the Strangest Stories of Crime in the City's History—Mr. Koesters's Young Son Fatally Injured—The Girl's Arrest

Indiana State Sentinel, Wednesday, May 31, 1893

A List of the Dead

Mary Koesters, the thirty-one-year-old wife of Charles, died October 15, 1892; the couple's three-month-old son, Charles, died January 6, 1893; Koesters's father Frank, aged seventy-four, died later that month on January 29 and was shortly followed to the grave by Mary Koesters, aged eight, on February 27. Clara, Koesters's mother, died on May 24. Each of them, except the baby, was ill for about the same length of time and showed the same violent and painful symptoms.

Quoting a line from Edgar Allen Poe's "The Raven," "when unmerciful disaster followed fast and followed faster," a news reporter observed how with five family members dead from supposed poison and another child dying from an accident, this "is the load of sorrow under which Charles Koesters rests today."

Another Death

Two days after the death of Charles Koesters's mother, seventy-three-year-old Clara Koesters, James, the six-year-old son of Charles and Mary, was thrown from a horse and killed.

A SON GROWS SUSPICIOUS

Green Bay Press-Gazette (WI), Saturday, May 27, 1893

"I suspected nothing until my little girl died on February 27 and then my suspicions were aroused by the statements of other people," said Koesters. "My father and mother-in-law thought there might be something wrong when my mother died with the same symptoms so suddenly. George Borst, druggist, sent for me and told me that Annie Wagner employed by me, had been in his store Monday morning May 21 and had bought a box of rat poison. Then I became alarmed and demanded a thorough investigation."

Borst said that Annie Wagner had said that she wanted the poison to kill rats with as they had eaten up a peck of apples. "She never said anything about rat poison; has not in the last three months said anything to me about there being rats or mice in the house. I have never heard of any apples being eaten up by rats. I have never seen a rat in the house I have seen mice. Annie Wagner cooked some of my mother's meats when she was sick."

His father had been fine the day before he became ill; so had his mother, Mamie, and the baby.

Koesters added that he thought Annie Wagner was in love with him, and he furnished the motive for the crime, suggesting that she wanted to get his wife and children out of the way to make room for him to marry her.

After his mother's death, Koesters began investigating and found poison in the cupboard.

> Wednesday morning a well-dressed German, apparently about thirty-five years of age, called at the coroner's office. He said his name was Charles Koesters and that lived at 556 S. Meridian Street. He had a strange story to relate, the substance of which was that he believed a domestic in his employ named Annie Wagner was responsible for the death of five members of his family, his wife, two children and his father and mother. Every death had occurred since October 15, 1892.

Charles wasn't the only one who thought the deaths were suspicious as he soon found out.

HAD BOUGHT ROUGH ON RATS

Indiana State Sentinel, **Wednesday, May 31, 1893**

> The coroner had, in the meantime, been making an investigation and upon inquiry in the neighborhood, had learned that the girl had purchased a 15 cent box of Rough on Rats at Borat's drugstore, a few doors from Koester's house.

Now working with Koesters, they wanted to perform an autopsy on Clara Koesters who was still in a coffin in an upstairs room of the Koesters's home.

> They were confronted by a serious obstacle however. A number of the relatives had gathered at the house and it was impossible to hold the autopsy without their knowledge. Mr. Koesters was

consulted in the matter and he informed the best time to do this work would be at an early hour yesterday morning.

About 1 o'clock Thursday morning the coroner and the two physicians called at the family residence, which is over the furniture store. When they arrived they were met at the door by Koesters who informed them that two of his relatives were upstairs and they insisted, in spite of his protests, of sitting up with the corpse. On the pretense of taking them to the Spencer house to get a cigar the men were gotten out of the house and the autopsy was held, the stomach removed.

By noon, Dr. Eisenbeiss told Coroner Manker what everyone suspected. There was enough arsenic in the fifth Koester stomach to be examined to cause death.

Ann Wagner's Movements on May 22

Charles Koesters was asked whether, to his knowledge, Anna Wagner had gone out the morning of May 22. He said:

She always went out in the morning. She must have gone out because she got meat that day. But I want to find out whether she had been out on that because you know, that is the day that Borst says she bought poison from him. We buy our meat from Vixler's meat market on McCarty Street and I asked him, and he said he did not know whether she had bought any from him that day or not. I asked his boys who in the store sometimes and they said they had not seen her that day. I went out to deliver some good at 10 o'clock and she might have gone out while I was away. I could not swear she was out of that morning at all.

Mary's sister was asked whether Annie ever fed the baby. Mrs. Ohleyer replied that she was at her home nearly every day.

She used to come here and sit in the front room with the babe and I was in the backroom. The feed bottle used to be in the cradle with the child. We used to feed it on condensed milk. The child was always sick. It was bad when we first took it (meaning after Mary's death) and it just seemed to grow less every day. The child died on Friday, the 26th of January. I don't know whether Annie Wagner was in to see it the day before but I think she was, in the morning. The child was always restless. It went to sleep and was dead in the morning. It was alive at 2:30 in the morning because we were awake and heard it move. Annie never fed it in this house but she used to take it over to the other house and I don't know what she did with it there. Of course we never suspected anything.

Annie Is Arrested

On the evidence accumulated, police entered the house and made their way to Wagner's bedroom to arrest her. At the time of her arrest, the prisoner denied having any poison in her possession, although the half emptied box was afterward found in the closet where she kept her clothes. But this poison was for bedbugs. The Rough on Rats brand of rat poison was found on a shelf in the kitchen where almost everyone in the house would have had access to it. That poison, she told them, she had gotten from her sister before Christmas.

She was taken to the drug store where the poison was bought and she denied to Druggist Borst ever having bought any Rough on Rats from him.

After a hearing in the police court on Tuesday, June 25, which lasted a few days, Annie Wagner was awarded bail, and within a few days had furnished the security required and was taken to her sister and brother-in-law's house. There she remained until the grand jury met and returned an indictment against her for murder in the first degree. She was rearrested and taken to jail without the privilege of bail and there she would stay until the end of the trial.

The *Indiana State Sentinel* reported that Annie, though at first indifferent, became depressed, spending her time crying and reading the little prayer book some of her friends gave her.

She has scarcely slept and all night long her prayers and sobs can be heard all over the place. Her sorrow and confinement if beginning to tell on her and her friends say that she has changed considerably since her arrest. Turnkey Collins, fearing that she would become seriously ill, sent a physician in to see her yesterday morning and he reported that her condition was good and he thought there was no danger of her becoming ill enough to take to her bed. She does not take her meals regularly with apparent relish. She still denies the charges against her and tells exactly the same story every day as the one on the day she was arrested.

No Femme Fatale

One newspaper described Annie Wagner as an ignorant German girl but news accounts also talked about her stoicism, calmness, and the way her story never changed. In appearance, she seems to have been neither dainty nor pretty, traits which had served other women on trial for murder well but instead "was above medium height, rather heavy build of dark complexion and angular features."

Born near Konigsberg in East Prussia, Wagner had come to Indianapolis accompanied by her sister, Mrs. John Burgman, five years before the murders. She first worked at Mueller's boarding house on South Alabama Street for nineteen months and said she left that job because Mrs. Mueller objected to her going to church. She next worked for Herman Francis and then, after going to live with her sister, found employment with the Koesters.

As for the deaths, Annie said that Mr. Koesters's father had been feeling badly for some time before he was taken to bed. Mamie also had been feeling unwell and had not eaten anything on the day she was taken sick. Coming home from school, she did consume a quantity of cheese that Annie thought was poisoned and caused her death.

Why Did She Do It?

The prosecution asserted that Annie Wagner, a stolid and solid German girl with a heavy accent, had set her cap for Charles Koesters even before his wife Mary, age thirty-one, died. Getting rid of a rival makes sense in a macabre sort of way. But then why destroy so many more family members?

Here are some of the reasons mentioned during the trial:

Frank and Clara Koesters lived behind the store at 417 Meridian Street, but after Mary's death, Charles asked them to move in with him. One reason was that he didn't think it proper to have a single woman (Annie) living in the house where there were no older adults. According to a witness, Annie found Frank a bother and having two more adults in the house difficult.

Frank Koesters, in his final illness, had written a will. According to Charles Koesters, he had about $5,000 or $6,000, properties on Union Street, and one on Meridian where he lived. About a year before his death, Frank had deeded Charles the Meridian Street property with the stipulation that he pay his father $24 every three months until he died. Then the property went to Clara Koesters who unfortunately drank some coffee Annie made for her and became sick, vomiting frequently, and having an unquenchable thirst.

Alarmed, Charles Koesters called a doctor who came to the house, examined his mother, and said everything was okay. After the doctor left, so did Koesters because he had a furniture delivery on the other side of town. Annie was left alone with the sick woman.

"Mother made her will the same day she died," Charles Koesters would testify later. "Her will read that I was to keep on paying her the $8 a month until she then died and then the property was to be mine, everything else was left to my brother Frank except for $100 each to the children when they came of age. Annie Wagner did not know anything about this will unless my mother told her."

Besides the money that Koesters would gain from his parents' death, there was another reason offered for why Annie thought Clara Koesters had to go. Clara was not her friend, often telling Charles that Annie acted too much like a boss. His father was upset when Annie served Charles first, saying that he should be served first and not be treated like "a step-child."

Margaret O'Lear, who came to the house on Tuesday afternoon and stayed about an hour, said that Clara was doing much better.

However, after Annie went upstairs to care for her, she died shortly thereafter.

According to an *Indianapolis News* story that ran on December 8, 1893, Mary Koesters's mother, Mrs. George Ohleyer who was taking care of the baby after her sister's death, recalled telling Annie Wagner to be good to the children and treat them kindly, adding "you may be the mistress of the house yourself sometime."

Annie was mostly silent after Mrs. Ohleyer's remark, though she said that Mr. Koesters objected to second marriages, and he had no need of getting married as long as his mother was alive since she could be counted on to take care of the family. So, if Annie wanted to marry Koesters, it makes sense that Clara had to go.

Mrs. Ohleyer also told the jury about Annie's dislike for Charles Koesters's parents: "Anna complained of the old man. She said that he wanted rabbits cooked in a particular way. Anna had a great deal of work to do. The old mother did much of the dishwashing herself."

Mrs. Mary Schmidt, another witness, testified that she had known Charles Koesters for eighteen years and was summoned to prepare Clara Koesters's body for burial.

Annie heated the water for them and gave them clothes after asking if they'd come to lay out the body. "Anna said, 'Oh, phew! the body does stink so. You'd better leave that to the undertakers,'" said Schmidt according to the *News* story. "Annie got some whisky then."

Charles Koesters testified that Annie Wagner often did things for him such as getting his slippers ready for him each evening, which other family members should be doing, and also that she wanted to be with him every possible moment.

Mamie, the eight year old, said she didn't like stepmothers and didn't want one. Thus it was Mamie's turn, though if you believe the defense, the context for Mamie's statement came after seeing a play about Snow White. Mamie then asked Annie if all stepmothers were mean. Annie supposedly said yes, that most of them were. To further increase Mamie's peril, Koesters's response to friends who were expressing their sympathy for him in his bereavement, remarked: "Well, my daughter Mamie is still left. Death has not taken her away, and she will soon be big enough to assume the duties of my household and comfort me."

Annie, who heard the remark, sharply responded, that no one could depend upon these little girls to do housework and that instead "You want a woman. These American girls can't be trusted and are too fond of running around."

Koesters, who obviously believed in a very patriarchal way of things, rejoined, saying that his daughter should have her dead mother's place. Within a week of this exchange, Mamie would be dead.

It does make one think, doesn't it?

There were other reasons to believe that Annie was in love with him, said Koesters. Notable was that Wagner made the children say they were "papa's and Annie's" children. She also offered to loan Koesters money, saying he'd had considerable funeral expenses, and that no one need know of the loan save themselves. The amounts she mentioned were $300 to $500, a considerable amount back then for a woman who was earning $3 a week as a servant.

After Mamie's death, Annie had spent large sums of money for flowers with which to decorate the casket. She also decorated the graves of both Mary and Mamie as well.

Annie attempted to stir Koesters's jealousy on St. Valentine's Day by having George Borst, the druggist, send two valentines to the house that were supposedly from an admirer. Nonchalantly saying she didn't like the sender, she gave the cards to one of the children.

These instances and more, said the prosecuting attorney, would prove that the defendant was carrying out a plan to get Koesters to marry her, adding that whether she loved Mr. Koesters or desired the marriage for the sake of bettering her condition was not material since first marriages only were for love and second marriages were for convenience.

Two Women Attempt to Force a Confession
from Annie Warner without Success

Two German ladies of South Meridian street, Mrs. Chris Birk and Mrs. John Schmitt, are inclined to the belief that Annie Wagner is resting under a dark and very suspicious cloud. They are intimate acquaintances of the Koesters family, and were in the house at diverse times during the illness of the inmates. They called at the jail yesterday, and, in conversation with Annie Wagner, discovered what they believed to be evidences of guilt. The interview was lengthy and heated, and resulted in the return of the girl to her cell much wrought up with emotion and, tears. One of the callers made an effort to extract a confession from the prisoner, but was met with the usual denial of guilt.

Mrs. Birk and Mrs. Schmitt both state that during the illness of the Koesters, Annie Wagner was assiduous in her attendance at the bedside, and would not consent to other persons interfering with her attention to the patients. They also recall another instance of the prisoner's strange actions in connection with the death of Mrs. Clara Koesters. Annie stood by and watched the women washing the dead body, and was requested to carry the water down stairs. She objected to touching the bowl with her hands, exclaiming vehemently that she "could never cook or eat again" if her hands came in contact with the vessel. Many other instances of the superstition or fear of harm to herself were related of Annie's demeanor.

The prosecution made much of Annie taking English lessons after Mary's death as another ploy to lure Charles into marriage, but wanting to marry a rich man is not a crime unless you clear the way by poisoning people.

Annie Takes the Stand

Taking the stand on December 18, Annie denied poisoning the family, saying that after Mrs. Koesters died and Charles was left a widower, he gave her the responsibility of looking after the children and their clothing because he knew nothing about doing such things. The attention she gave them was because they were motherless. As for Koesters, she took care of him because he was without a wife. She also continued to deny she had been in Borst's store the day he said she was. She told the courtroom that if Borst was a Catholic he would not say she was in the store, alluding to his feelings about her and his tendency to be less than reliable with the truth.

When the police came to arrest her and asked about the rat poison, she said she had forgotten it was there and also did not understand what the officers were searching for.

Her sister, Mrs. Burgman, came forward and said she had indeed given Annie the rat poison three weeks before Christmas. Questioned as to why she hadn't told the officers that story when first asked by the police, Mrs. Burgman used a line similar to that of her sister. She misunderstood the question and thought they wanted to know if she had poisoned the girl or not, which of course she emphatically said she did not do.

Many seemed to admire Wagner because she gave her statements in front of the courtroom in a straightforward manner and without hesitation.

"There is one peculiar thing about Annie Wagner; when she fully understands the questions asked her, she at once makes an answer, and does so in ways that makes her listeners believe that she is telling the truth," wrote a reporter for the *Indiana State Sentinel*.

Annie's Hard Life

One part of the defense's strategy was to paint a picture of an overworked servant, a poor girl from Germany taken advantage of by her cruel boss.

Mr. Spaan, one of her attorneys, talked about the amount of sewing Annie had to do for the family.

Annie herself testified to her hard work and the toll it took on her.

"I was always tired every night, every night," she said.

Spaan then mentioned that, at Koesters's request, Annie paid for the family's washing, and that the money had never been paid back and never would be.

He lauded her abilities in taking care of the children (or at least the ones who were left), saying they knew she was the one who kept them clean and with happy faces and how they went to her and not the money-making man who thought that fifteen cents of wienerwurst for the family was enough. He also lauded Annie for paying for presents for the children and for flowers for the graves of Mary and her daughter Mamie.

But Koesters wasn't the hardest of bosses. When Annie told him her pay should be cut to $2 a week instead of the $3 he was paying because she was away at school so much, Koesters insisted on keeping her salary the same.

The Tides Turn in Annie's Favor

Charles Koesters didn't do well on the stand despite the horrific tragedies he'd endured.

Annie's attorneys were able to paint her as an overworked servant who gave her all for the family, motivated not because of designs on Charles Koesters, but because of her love of the children and her duty.

"Many persons who have interested themselves in the case of the Koesters family are now beginning to express doubts as to the guilt of Annie Wagner," wrote one reporter. "Attorney Frank Mattler was first engaged for the defense of Annie Wagner, and after a thorough consultation with the accused and a close investigation of the facts and evidence has been brought to light, is firm in the belief of her innocence."

JURORS SHED TEARS

Anna Wagner's Testimony Proves Remarkably Affecting

Sterling Standard (IL), Thursday, December 21, 1893

The evidence of Anna Wagner, accused of poisoning the Koesters family, was of a pathetic nature than any given in the trial. She broke into tears repeatedly and the eyes of the jurymen were noticed to be swimming with tears repeatedly, while the women among the spectators were decidedly affected by the young woman's story.

Great sympathy is being expressed for the innocent-appearing prisoner and there is a surmise that Judge Cox at the close of the trial may even instruct the jury to bring in a verdict of acquittal without leaving the box. Miss Wagner's testimony yesterday was most convincing, and there are not wanting persons who believe the charges against her were made for the purpose of covering up a crime committed by Koesters himself.

Oh yes, the defense attempted to get jurors to believe that Charles Koesters murdered his family. Why?

Daily Review (Decatur, IL), **Wednesday, December 20, 1893**

Charles Baden of Milwaukee Brewing company testified to the frequent quarrels between Charles Koesters and his broth in regard to the disposition of their father's property.

Attorney Spann stated to the jury after Baden left the stand that he proposed to show that the lives of the dead members of the family stood in the way of the brothers gaining the estate and that there was a motive on their part in desiring to get rid of them. Charles Koesters is the chief witness against the girl.

FINDING A MOTIVE

The Defense in the Anna Wagner Trial Doing Well

———————

A Midnight Call on a Notary

———————

Who Made a Will for Old Man Koesters
That Did Not Suit His Sons

Logansport Pharos-Tribune, **Tuesday, December 19, 1893**

Charles Boden, who was a notary public, arrived at the Koesters house around midnight about two months before their father died, called there by Frank and Charles Koesters who wanted him to draw up a will. Boden testified that the brothers quarreled in the sickroom over the division of property until finally their father intervened. "The provisions of the will were very unsatisfactory to both, and attorney Spaan stated to the jury that he proposed to show that the lives of the dead members of the family stood in the way of the brothers gaining the estate."

Then Annie caught another break, unless you cynically believe that someone was paid to provide her an alibi.

RESEMBLED THE PRISONER: FORTUNATE CIRCUMSTANCE FOR ANNIE WAGNER TURNS UP

Oshkosh Daily (WI), **Tuesday, June 13, 1893**

Interest in the case of Annie Wagner, charged with the poisoning of five members of the family of Charles Koesters, a prominent German furniture dealer, was heightened yesterday that a young woman named Annie Watsky, and greatly resembling the Wagner girl, said the she bought rat poison on the day that Borst says he sold it to Annie Wagner. Miss Watsky lives on Chadwick Street and according to her story, she went to Borst store on the Monday that the Koesters had their picnic and there bought the rat poison. Today she called at the jail and had a long talk with Annie Wagner in which she said that she believed it was a case of mistaken identity and that it was herself and not the Wagner girl that bought the poison. The friends of the prisoner are growing in numbers every day and believe she will be released.

As Annie's star waxed, Koesters, who was not a warm and fuzzy kind of guy, became alarmed at the turn of the trial was taking, with Wagner's attorneys suggesting that maybe he and his brother Frank had committed the murders.

Koesters appeared to be much worried over the turn affairs are taking and as he rose, said "This talk about property, what's it for? I know they suspect me. They hint around and try and find out about this and that. I will tell you anything I can. What should I kill my little girl for; she's got no money. Oh, this is terrible, terrible. It hurts my business, too, and people who don't to think, think bad of me."

ANNIE WAGNER, A "SYMPATHETIC" INDIANA SERIAL KILLER WHO GOT AWAY WITH MURDER

Morning Herald (Baltimore, MD), **Friday, December 8, 1893**

Annie Wagner was acquitted. The impression made by this result in light of the evidence was that "not guilty" was a nullification verdict due to jurors' sympathy for Annie because of her claim of self-sacrifice in her capacity as a caregiver to motherless children. The evidence nevertheless supports the charges that she was a serial killer.

On December 28, after being out for twelve hours, the jury in Annie Wagner's murder case brought in a verdict of not guilty. The courtroom was crowded, and the announcement of the verdict was received with cheer after cheer. During a scene of the wildest confusion, the prisoner fainted away. Throughout the trial Annie Wagner manifested the most stoical indifference, and it was not until the verdict of the jury that her feelings obtained mastery over her. Mr. Holtzman, the prosecutor, announced that as the state had failed to convict in this, its best case, and owing to the state of public opinion, he deemed it best to dismiss the other two indictments for murder against the prisoner. "Not since the trial of Mrs. Nancy Clem for the murder of Jacob Young and wife as at Cold Springs, north of this city, twenty years ago, has the Indianapolis public been as much interested in a murder trial as in the case which has just closed."

Annie had become somewhat of a celebrity and after being released and moving into her sister's home, women would stop by, telling her they'd never lost faith in her and giving her their photos.

Koesters on the other hand thought she should have been convicted, but he too was stoic. When asked in the office of his furniture store what he thought of the verdict, he said, "What can I think? It is done. I cannot help it."

The reporters noted he became emotional several times and had to wipe tears from his eyes, saying he supposed he would have to stand it.

Rough on Rats

One of the most commonly used arsenic-based rat poisons, Rough on Rats was introduced to the market in the 1860s and continued in popularity until the late 1920s. The box displayed a drawing of a dead rat lying on its back (proof that the product worked). At one time the tag line was "The old reliable don't die in the house." Because arsenic was not only deadly for rats but also other animals as well as humans, new raticides were introduced in the late 1920s. But even before that, better sanitation conditions as well as a change in building practices where concrete was used more than wood particularly for foundations were helping limit the rat population.

Author's note: Though it seems, from reading contemporary news accounts, that many thought Annie Wagner guilty, somehow her working-class roots and the rigid, fastidious personality of Charles Koesters and his father (the one who demanded he be served first at dinner instead of his son because otherwise he felt as though he was being treated as a stepchild), struck a chord with the women who followed the trial. Maybe some of them yearned for a little Rough on Rats for their husbands as well. But their interest also caused a backlash of sorts as shown by the following article. It seems some men didn't feel comfortable with a woman supposedly using arsenic somewhat indiscriminately to gain her matrimonial goals or that any woman, no matter her situation in life, should support a fellow female who had indulged in such an endeavor.

FEMININE CURIOSITY

Indiana State Sentinel, **Wednesday, December 13, 1893**

> The morbid curiosity which calls itself sympathy and interest has broken out in an alarming degree in the case of Annie Wagner trial. . . . As in the case of Minnie Mabbitt, who was tried for

murder, women are rushing to the court-room in great crowds fairly knocking each other down in their eagerness to see the prisoner and hear every detail. Strange to say, it is the women with families and household duties who seem to take the greatest interest in the case and who leave their husbands and children motherless to attend the trial.

In fact, one poor man was so overcome at having to wait for dinner that he went to the court-room and cried, either because he could not get inside on account of the crowd or because he wanted to spoil his wife's fun. . . . They act more like a set of children just out of school than like intelligent human beings with any attribute save that of curiosity. They bring opera-glasses to watch the face of the prisoner who, fortunately, does not seem to mind them, and they giggle and laugh over every tilt between the lawyers as if the whole affair was some huge joke.

Nor do the women who attend the trial belong wholly to the class supposed to enjoy sensations. Ladies from the wealthy resident portion of the city, women of apparent refinement rub elbows with women of the street.

Hmmm . . . pass the Rough on Rats please.

7

The Disappearance of Carrie Selvage

Indianapolis Star, Saturday, August 8, 1903

When officers removed the last shovelfuls of dirt covering the graves at Union Chapel Cemetery and pried open the two caskets, they believed one of them would finally reveal what had happened to the long-missing Carrie Selvage.

Authorities were relying on the statements of Rufus Cantrell, dubbed by the press as the King of the Ghouls. Cantrell headed a gang of grave robbers who scoured Indianapolis cemeteries, digging up those freshly buried to sell to medical schools. Rufus had many careers including a year in the Twenty-Fourth U.S. Infantry. But it was his stint working as an assistant for Cassius M. C. Willis, the first African American undertaker and funeral director in Indiana, that may have introduced Rufus into the lucrative world of cadavers.

A member of a wealthy Indianapolis family, Selvage was a school teacher who served as secretary in such prestigious social organizations as the Ladies Aid and the Wesley United Methodist Church; she also was the president of the Hyperion Club. How Selvage, a delicate 118-pound woman with such prestigious connections, could end up in a grave that Cantrell had already once robbed was a big mystery.

But life had started to unravel for Selvage, who not only was delicate in size but at this point in her life, frail in nature. She'd suffered a nervous breakdown and her family, wanting the best for her, had gone to the trouble and expense to make her stay at the Union State Hospital as comfortable as possible by enlarging the front room.

Before becoming a hospital offering private treatments for those suffering from mental and nervous disorders, the pre–Civil War era building at 1332 North Capitol Avenue in Indianapolis had originally housed the Indianapolis Orphan Asylum, a place said to be haunted by the children buried in unmarked graves. Perhaps, one might argue, not quite the place for people who already suffered from nervous dispositions.

Supposedly comfy and cossetted in the hospital setting, Selvage would seem to be as far away from the *rampaging ghouls,* a Middle Eastern term meaning eaters of the dead, who raided city cemeteries at night.

Grave robbing was serious and macabre problem of the nineteenth century. According to "The Harrison Horror, Grave Robbing and the Invention of the Burial Vault 1878" by Todd W. Van Beck in the Indiana Funeral Directors Association publica-

The Indianapolis home of William Henry Harrison, grandson of a U.S. president and the son of a U.S. senator. Even the pedigree of this high-achievement family didn't protect them from the rampant grave robbing that was epidemic in the late 1800s. Photo courtesy of Jane Simon Ammeson.

tion, even two U.S. presidents became entangled in grave robbing plots.

After the burial of Ohio Senator John Scott Harrison, as mourners began leaving the Harrison family plot and vault in the Congress Green Cemetery on the Ohio River near Cincinnati, someone noticed the gravesite of young Augustus Devin had been disturbed, and his body appeared to be missing. Among the mourners was Devin's uncle and John Scott's son, Benjamin Harrison, an Indianapolis attorney who some nineteen years later would become the twenty-third president of the United States. Benjamin's grandfather, William Henry Harrison, was the nation's ninth president and as the governor of the Indiana territory had led the battle of Tippecanoe in 1811 against a confederacy of Indians living near Lafayette, Indiana. In other words, the twenty-three-year-old Devin was well connected and robbing his grave had been a big mistake as the family had the resources and clout to hunt down the robbers.

According to Van Beck, Harrison and his family worked quickly to make sure Devin's widowed mother didn't learn of the body's disappearance. They also took the precautionary step of safeguarding John Scott Harrison's grave.

> To this end Benjamin Harrison together with his younger brother John supervised the actual lowering of his father's body into an eight-foot-long grave. At the bottom, as a secure receptacle for the metallic casket was a brick vault with thick walls and a stone bottom. Three flat stones, eight or more inches thick were procured for a cover. With great difficulty the stones were lowered over the casket, the largest at the upper end and the two smaller slabs crosswise at the foot. All three were carefully cemented together. For several hours the grave was left open so that the cement might dry. Finally, under guard a great quantity of dirt was shoveled over the stones.

One might think that would be enough. But alas, it wasn't. After most of the family had returned home, and Benjamin Harrison to Indianapolis, his brother John and cousin George Eaton obtained a search warrant and accompanied by two law men, started their search for Devin's body at the Ohio Medical College. Their reasons for beginning there were twofold. One, body snatchers often sold the purloined goods to medical schools, and two, they'd been told at 3 o'clock that morning a wagon had stopped in front of the college door where remains were typically delivered and something had been removed from the wagon before it again rattled away down the street.

Though Harrison and Eaton believed Devin's body most likely had been sold earlier in the week, the police suggested trying the college.

Going room to room, the group found nothing, not even in the chute where bodies were dumped after being dissected. Writes Van Beck,

At last when the building had been thoroughly searched, young John and George were ready to look elsewhere. Constable Lacey, however, noticed a taut rope attached to the windlass. Immediately he ordered Detective Snelbaker to haul it up. It was not an easy task for as the windlass was pulled it was soon evident that there was a heavy weight at the end of the rope. At last there emerged into the light a body. A cloth covered only the head and shoulders of what appeared to be the body of a very old man.

Because Devin was young, Harrison wasn't much interested in the discovery until Lacey, using a stick, removed the cloth covering the man.

"As he did so, Harrison caught sight of the dead man's face and exclaimed in horror that the dead body was none other than that of his father, John Scott Harrison."

In a coincidence almost too melodramatic to believe—though it really happened—relatives of John Scott Harrison, visiting his grave discovered two of the smaller stones originally placed across the outer coffin had been lifted on end, holes had been drilled in the outer coffin, the lid of the inner coffin had been pried open, the glass seal had been broken, and the body had been drawn out feet first.

"This was contrary to the usual practice of body snatching," writes Van Beck, "indicating that one of the perpetrators had been present at the burial and had noted that the smaller stones were placed over the foot of the vault."

Carter Harrison and Archie Eaton quickly hurried to Cincinnati to find their siblings.

"When they met, Carter Harrison informed the others that John Scot Harrison's body had been stolen while at the same time John Harrison informed the others that he had discovered the body of John Scott Harrison."

Go figure.

But now the story becomes even stranger. The family continued to search for Devin's body and finally got a clue when professors from both the Ohio Medical College and Miami Medical College admitted they had contracts guaranteeing them an annual supply of bodies. Further questioning revealed Cincinnati was a cadaver distribution center that parceled out cadavers, some in barrels, to smaller cities such as Ann Arbor, Michigan. Police headed to the medical college there and on finding barrels labeled Quimby and Co., they checked the delivery dates, found one close to the time Devin's body had been stolen and finally located him in a pickling brine. According to HistoricIndianapolis.com, "In Michigan and northern Indiana, grave robbing was worst in towns close to the Michigan Central Railroad and its branch lines, since bodies could quickly be hidden on trains and shipped as freight to Ann Arbor's famous medical school."

It was a rainy day when Devin returned home four weeks to the day after he had been stolen from his grave, but a large crowd turned out to watch him be buried again.

"Long after the funeral cortege had left the scene there remained around the sacred enclosure a volunteer guard composed entirely of citizens," writes Van Beck. "This was a practice instituted the night after the robbery of John Scott Harrison's grave. No precaution was overlooked. Even citizens late in getting home at night were halted by their self-appointed sentries."

As far as Indianapolis was concerned, there seemed to be more bodies above ground than under in the early 1900s. At most, around 1902, some 315 bodies were snatched from their graves.

Physicians accompanied them (the resurrectionists as body snatchers were also known) on several of their night trips. It has been shown in the disclosures that the body of the wife of one of the ghouls was sold by the undertaker to a college. Cantrell, the chief ghoul, drove the empty coffin in a hearse to a roadhouse near the cemetery with no escort, stopped, got drunk and boasted of the empty coffin which he showed.

Ten bodies were found buried beneath a few inches of earth in the basement of one of the colleges, four bodies were found in sacks on the streets, where the hard-pressed ghouls had dropped

The Gothic entrance gates and high stone walls at the historic 555-acre Crown Hill Cemetery, where Carrie Selvage now rests, were designed that way just for aesthetics. At one time, armed guards even walked the perimeter of the cemetery to prevent grave robbing. Photo courtesy of Marty N. Davis.

Crown Hill Cemetery, founded in 1863, is a lovely stretch of land with thickets of trees, elaborate tombstones and mausoleums, and a grand Gothic chapel all set amid a gently rolling landscape. Photo courtesy of Marty N. Davis.

Mary Ella McGinnis, born December 15, 1869; died August 6, 1875, of lung congestion. Her statue is located in section 16, lot 23, Crown Hill Cemetery, and is considered one of the cemetery's best known statues. Photo courtesy of Marty N. Davis.

them, one body was concealed for two days in a saloon, and in the search for bodies stolen from local cemeteries, thirty were found in cold storage in an ice cream factory at Louisville. The grand jury will return another bunch of indictments later. (*Inter Ocean* [Chicago, IL], October 26, 1902)

Cantrell liked to boast about the tricks of their trade. Sometimes coffins were emptied before they even made it to the graveyard, their mortal remains removed and blocks of ice substituted instead. Grave robbers posed as grave diggers, barely waiting for families to leave before getting to work. Interesting to note, plots decorated with elaborate floral displays often were deterrents for resurrectionists as it was too difficult and took too much time to return them to their original condition—necessary to avoid signaling the body was gone.

According to Joan Hostetler, an Indianapolis historian and former Indiana State Museum researcher, Cantrell, a would-be preacher since his teens, performed the ceremony at his niece's funeral in the afternoon and later that night dug up her corpse and sold it. Because time was of the essence, Hostetler says resurrectionists dug up just one end of a casket, smashing the lid at the end and, using a hook they attached to the corpse, it was pulled out of the hole they'd made. Then, they'd put the coffin back and fill up the hole.

Of course, like many black market enterprises, it was the demand for bodies that made body snatching—obviously a distasteful job—so rewarding. Compare $35 to $50 for one body to the typical wage of about $426 a year for a manufacturing job and you can see that a competent resurrection man (I use the word man because in all my research I never read about a woman grave digger) could turn nine bodies into a salary equal to a year's wages for the average laborer. Medical colleges needed bodies to dissect in order to turn out well-trained physicians and dentists. Laws against using cadavers created an—excuse the pun—underground market. But it was the men who did the dirty work such as Rufus and his gang (there were also rival gangs of body snatchers in Indy and they at times came to blows, even killing each other and then selling their dead rivals to schools) who went to jail while the doctors were rarely punished.

With all this going on, on the night of March 11, 1900, Selvage went missing. Her nurse had left the hospital to run a quick errand, leaving Selvage in a long blue flannelette wrapper with felt house slippers on her feet. Not exactly the right outfit to be wearing outside on a cold late winter evening.

Her family along with the private detectives they hired, the police, and Carrie's friends conducted what the *San Francisco Chronicle,* in a June 13, 1920 article described as a "most systematic search for her. Every possible clue was traced to its end. Ponds and lakes, Fall Creek and White River were dragged. Copies of her photographs together with descriptive personal details were broadcast without success. The young school teacher had vanished."

It was then that Rufus stepped forward with his story—or rather stories as they had some differences though overall the general gist was the same. On trial for his crimes, he recalled that on that date in 1900, he and his gang were doing what they did many nights, haunting cemeteries for freshly buried bodies to dig up and sell to medical schools.

According to an article on Saturday, August 8, 1903, in the *Indianapolis Star,* Cantrell signed an affidavit saying he and another man were driving in a buggy from Southport to Indianapolis over the Madison Road.

> When we reached the Belt crossing we met a woman coming toward us. She was bareheaded and wore a loose blue wrapper. She was of medium size, slender, white and had brown hair. This hair I later sold to a milliner near the corner of Washington and Pennsylvania streets, in Indianapolis.
>
> It was about noon when we met her, the other man spoke to her. She asked him to take her home. She talked in a sort of foolish way; didn't seem to have any home and at his invitation she got into the buggy.
>
> He then drove me home and took the woman to Westfield the same evening. He had a house in Westfield where this woman was kept for several weeks.

This woman's name, I believe, was Selvage. After she had been kept at the house at Westfield two or three weeks, he became afraid of discovery and she was brought to my home in Indianapolis.

Rufus denied participating in the murder of the woman but someone identified him as taking the woman's body and putting it in a barrel, which was then delivered to a dental college.

Years later, when in Detroit, Cantrell's story morphed slightly. In this version, Selvage showed up at a cemetery they were robbing, scaring his men. She stood there, the King of the Ghouls said, in her nightgown and slippers, her hair wild. He claimed to have taken her to a basement where he killed her (in another story he found her in the basement with her throat slit) and sold her body to the Indiana Medical College.

In another variation, Selvage showed up at the cemetery gate and the ghouls overpowered her to so she couldn't give the alarm about what they were doing. They'd taken her to a basement on Indiana Avenue where she had died three days later. Not wanting to waste a good body, they sold her to a medical clinic for $50.

And then there was his story of finding Selvage on the morning after her disappearance wandering a country road. Taking her into their buggy, the ghouls discovered she was demented and drove her to a cabin in Hamilton where she was kept for weeks before being moved to a hut in Indianapolis. When searchers came too close, the woman was chloroformed and her body buried at the Union Chapel Cemetery.

It was this latter story that led the police and Selvage's brother to unearth coffins in the hopes of finding Selvage's body. Cantrell couldn't remember the exact grave but said it was one that had been disturbed, the rough box broken up and coffin lid overturned. And that's what they found, only, according to Carrie's brother, it wasn't her body. They dug further, searching other graves but none contained the body they were looking for.

During the years Selvage remained missing, Cantrell was busy and his trials and exploits garnered both a lot of press and jail time.

He and several of his fellow ghouls were tried and sentenced to ten years in prison but by 1909 Cantrell was free and working at the American Steel and Wire Company in Anderson, Indiana. But he didn't stay at it very long.

"KING OF GHOULS"

Negro Rufus Cantrell Will Do Vaudeville Stunts in Indiana When on Parole

Cincinnati Enquirer, Tuesday, August 16, 1910

Anderson, Ind. August 15—Rufus Cantrell, a negro, sent from Indianapolis to State Prison 10 years ago for grave robbing, has turned to vaudeville while on parole in this city.

About a year ago, Cantrell was paroled and a local steel mill where Cantrell is employed, reports to the Parole Boards as to Cantrell's conduct. Recently when Cantrell became involved in a family row, resulting in officers taking a hand. Cantrell pleaded for suppression of his name or any reference to his past, declaring he was trying to live down his past.

It seems now that the lure of the Vaudeville stage has lifted Cantrell's play from oblivion and he will go before the footlights. A local vaudeville is advertising Cantrell as "Rufus Cantrell, the famous king of the ghouls," in a great lecture on his past horrible life.

It also is announced that three other members of the famous ghouls will appear.

Always flamboyant and always in trouble with the law, Rufus surfaces again on Christmas Eve 1915 when he headed to Flint, Michigan, after being charged for running a *blind tiger*, a term for a speakeasy or illegal bar. In Flint, he ran a revival using an assumed name. On the other side of the Detroit River in Windsor, Ontario, he got married. Later he was arrested and sent to the Marquette Prison in 1916 for two years; he disappears from history around 1920.

DUTED
ONIANS
C BATTLE

ed of the Insur-
Back in Confu-
Battalions of
i's Troops.

ILLED THE
IONIST FORCES

attle Follows a
'shes and the
Triumphed.

BREAK IS
BE PREMATURE

Hundred Mace-
'eported to Be

CONFESSED A SERIES OF REVOLTING MURDERS

RUFUS CANTRELL MAKES NEW
CONFESSION TO MANY MURDERS

He Gives Complete Details of Crimes
Which Have Heretofore Been Re-
garded as Complete Mysteries and
Which the Police Have Been Unable to Solve.

GHOUL MAKES OATH
WHILE IN PRISON

Tells of Murder of Policeman Watterson; a Colored
Man Named Walter Johnson; an Unknown
Man Whose First Name Was Claude; a Negro
Called Jim, and Carrie Selvage--Cantrell Says
He Makes Voluntary Confession of the Crimes
--Gives the Names of Murderers.

Newspaper story about the King of Ghouls, Rufus Cantrell. Newspapers.com.

San Francisco Chronicle, **Sunday, June 13, 1920**

As if the disappearing Carrie and the grave robbers wasn't strange enough, when writing a summary of the case, the Sunday, June 13, 1920, edition of the *San Francisco Chronicle* reported that shortly after Selvage disappeared, medical students had assembled around an operating table for a dissection demonstration of the body of a young woman. One student noted her face looked similar to newspaper photographs of Carrie Selvage. Others agreed and after a discussion, one student suggested contacting a dentist friend of his who had done dental work for Selvage. The dentist thought that yes, the gold fillings possibly looked like his work. 'Taking into consideration her nervous breakdown, exposure, and death, Selvage's brother thought it might be her as well. But after further consideration, the clothes on the body at the time of her delivery weren't the ones Carrie was wearing when she disappeared. It wasn't Carrie they finally decided, and the body was removed from the table and given a decent burial. Whether it was dug up again and resold isn't known.

In 1920, the old Union Hospital, now abandoned, was scheduled to be demolished when iron construction worker Dan Jones climbed to the top of a small and barely accessible cupola atop the brick building.

Enlarging the opening, Jones managed to get his head into the room and found himself, unpleasantly enough, face to face with a headless standing skeleton. Other accounts have the skeleton sitting in a chair, but either way it was a skeleton dressed in the remains of a blue wrapper and felt house sleepers whose head had fallen to the floor and rolled to one side. In other words, it most likely was Carrie Selvage. After all that searching it turned out she had never left the hospital two decades ago.

Carrie's brothers, Joseph and Edward, identified the slippers as a pair they'd given her a short time before she vanished. The wrapper also belonged to her.

Dr. Paul E. Robinson, coroner, said the skeleton was that of a young woman though he couldn't determine whether she'd been carried to the attic or whether she went there of her own accord. There was no evidence of violence, he said. Carrie might have starved to death but because March 11, 1900, was a bitterly cold evening and the attic full of drafts, it seemed more likely she'd frozen to death.

Joseph Selvage recalled how he and his brother had search the building after their sister disappeared but they've never heard of the small upper or second attic until twenty years later, when Jones discovered her body. Both brothers agreed that, unlike the woman on the dissecting table, this was Carrie Selvage.

Carrie was finally—and really—buried at the historic 555-acre Crown Hill Cemetery located at 700 West 38th Street in Indianapolis. Founded in 1863, it's a lovely stretch of land with thickets of trees, elaborate tombstones and mausoleums, a grand Gothic chapel all set amid a gently rolling landscape. Crown Hill is surrounded by a brick and wrought iron fence, erected in part, to protect the cemetery's residences. According to HistoricIndianapolis.com, "By 1902, Crown Hill had 24-hour security. Revolver-toting guards roamed the grounds, walking between a series of call boxes that required them to check in at different corners of the cemetery every 20 minutes."

By the time Carrie came to rest, the laws had changed and she was able to rest in peace.

8

NO WAY TO LEAVE YOUR LOVERS

AT 3 A.M. on April 28, 1908, in La Porte, Indiana, neighbors were awakened by the smell of smoke and the crackle of flames as they arched high in the sky consuming the farmhouse of Belle Gunness, a Norwegian widow with three young children.

Rushing to help and soon joined by townspeople, it took a while to put out the fast moving, intensely hot blaze, and by the time they did, much of Belle's home and many of the outbuildings had been destroyed. Searchers soon discovered the bodies—one was presumed to be the widow minus her head and the others her children—in the home's basement, all burned beyond immediate recognition.

Focus almost immediately turned to Ray Lamphere, a former farmhand hired by Mrs. Gunness, whom she had fired and prosecuted on charges of insanity. Lamphere, a gaunt and cadaverous looking man with really scary eyes, had threatened to get even with his boss, making him an even more likely suspect in what appeared to be arson and murder.

As awful as that seemed, the case quickly spiraled into an even more chilling and complex scenario. Noticing the dirt in several areas of the farm yard looked disturbed, authorities started

Ray Lamphere, Belle's handyman, was convicted of arson. He was dead a year later in prison. Photo courtesy of the La Porte County Historical Society.

digging and what they discovered would soon shock the nation. Andrew Helgelien, buried in a shallow grave in the kitchen garden, was the first body found in what would become known as Belle's cemetery. Another excavation revealed the bodies of two women. More digging turned up more graves, many of them filled with a jumble of gruesome body parts that didn't completely match up.

Like an archaeological dig, photographers recorded the scenes and their horrific finds. It's an amazingly awful set of photos showing badly decomposed bodies, teeth, torsos, legs, and arms. Body parts were everywhere—in the pig pen, among the ruin of the barn, on a hillside. It's easy to overuse "nightmarish," but in this case it was that and more.

"Here's the sluice, they found the teeth here," says Susie Richter, curator of the La Porte County Historical Society as she points to a photo, one of many on display at their museum, which has a whole section dedicated to Belle Gunness, local gal gone bad.

Though people flocked to the scene—pictures show women wearing long skirts and men in long overcoats standing in the mud and the snow, all wearing hats—it appears they were mostly able to prevent them from damaging the crime scene.

As the charred bodies, skeletons, and limbs were discovered, they were carefully transported in wagons to Cutler's Funeral Home in La Porte where they could be examined by a team of doctors.

In all, by the time they were done exhuming all the gravesites and attempting to assemble the pieces of corpses into completed human remains, authorities estimated that at least forty bodies had been buried along a peaceful country road in lovely La Porte County. But authorities soon realized, none of them belonged to Belle. Sure, the three children found in the basement were hers—and as they would soon learn killing children were among Belle's specialties. But the headless body wasn't Belle.

Belle with her children. Not the maternal type, none of Belle's children survived her. Photos courtesy of the La Porte County Historical Society.

Exhibit "B"

April 29, 1908

La Porte County Historical Society Archives

Joseph Maxson, being duly deposed as follows:

> I am hired man on Mrs. Gunness's place. Night before last I went to bed about half past eight. My room was over the kitchen. At the time I went to bed no one was in the house but Mrs. Gunness and her three children and myself. I soon went to sleep. . . . I think I was awakened by smell of smoke in the room. I heard the fire cracking and looked to see where I was. I opened my window; it opened eastward. I saw out the window that the east side of the brick part of the house was on fire and the east side of the frame part, in what part my room was, was burning. There was a door from my room into the brick part of the house. I tried to open this door—tried to kick it open. I could not succeed as it was fastened on the other side.

Maxson managed to get outside where he was soon joined by William Clifford and William Humphrey. Using a ladder, they peered into two of the second-story windows, but the beds were empty and no one was in either room.

Before they could search anymore, the intensity of the flames drove them back from the house. Maxson hitched up a wagon and drove into La Porte where he told Deputy Sheriff Anstiss about the fire. Maxson then headed back to the farm; Anstiss and Sheriff Smutzer, who had a car were already there.

"Almost all the walls had fallen in," said Maxson, describing what he saw upon his return. He would continue for hours to clear the debris, looking for Belle and the children until finally their bodies were found in basement.

Exhibit "F"

———————

May 20, 1908

La Porte County Historical Society Archives

Daniel M. Hutson, after duly being sworn in, testified that he had been awakened on the morning of the 28th when a neighbor came to his house and told him the Gunness house was on fire. He hurriedly dressed and when he got to there, saw the house was a "solid mass of fire."

After the arrival of the sheriffs, Hutson heard a group of people saying there was a queer smoke.

"It smelled bad," he said. "It smelled some of rags but it did not smell of lumber."

After going home for breakfast, Hutson returned to the farm.

"Mr. Smutzer told us to throw bricks," he testified. "We couldn't handle them; they were so hot. You can see still what those hot bricks did to my fingers. I went home to dinner. After dinner I worked the Gunness place until the bodies were found. I helped carry them into Undertaker Cutler's wagon."

On May 18, 1908, Dr. Franklin Silcox, a practicing physician in La Porte, made a postmortem examination of a body he determined, by its uterus, vagina, and shape of the pelvis, was a woman.

> The body was nude and in an advanced state of decomposition. . . . The right arm was severed by [illegible word in transcript] chopping instrument an inch below the head of the humerus. Both arms detached from the body. The two femurs were cut through the lower third. There were found four arms and four forearms with hands with the body but it is impossible to say which if any belong to this body. There were found two skulls and two lower maxillary bones with this body . . . there were also two sets of tibia and fibula that could not be positively identified as belonging to the body.

The digger opening the fifth grave found a pair of woman's Oxford tie shoes as well as another shoe and the metal frame of a woman's bag. "It looks as though this body, with its torso in a gunny sack, were perhaps enclosed in a box buried."

In the piles of depositions are the stories of some of the men whose relatives had tried desperately to find them. Among them is the tragic story of John O. Moe, Elbow Lake, Minnesota.

"My name is Jens G. Render. . . . My half-brother, the son of my mother, John O. Moe I last saw about January 2, 1906. He was a bachelor. He had been a subscriber to Skandinavian published in Chicago. December 22, 1906, he presented at the First National Bank in LaPorte for collection, a draft for $1000 drawn on the National Park Bank of New York and another draft for $100."

Render didn't learn about these withdrawals until May 13, 1908, but when he did he traveled to LaPorte and went to the First National Bank, showing a photo of his half-brother to Alfred Peglow, an assistant cashier, who immediately recognized John Moe and the transactions.

Peglow was eager to help and suggested that Render go to How's Jewelry Store to look for Moe's watch. From there he went to Sheriff Smutzer's office at the courthouse to identify the watch and then on to the office of Prosecuting Attorney R. N. Smith. Renders was able to identify the watch by its number.

Taken to view the bodies, Renders was unable to pick out Moe.

"But I feel entirely confident that he lost his life the Gunness place in Center Township, LaPorte County," he said.

Mat Budsberg came from Iola, Wisconsin, in search of his father whom he had last seen alive on April 5, 1907.

"He was, if living, a Norwegian," says Budsberg who had lived on a farm near Iola with his father, Ole O. Budsberg. "He spoke broken English. He took a Norwegian newspaper called *Skandianven* and another called *Decorah Posten* published in Decorah, Iowa. He left home April 5, 1907 to come to LaPorte and run a farm for Mrs. Gunness. . . . Before coming home, he had told his brother that he was going away to get married. When he left home he had with him, according to what the cashier of the bank said, about $800 in cash and a draft for $1000."

Though his father had promised to write when he reached the Gunness residence, the family never heard from him and began to worry. Budsberg and his brothers wrote to their father.

"Before my letter had come back to me through the dead letter office, a letter came from Mrs. Gunness, addressed to my father," related Budsberg who himself had traveled to LaPorte in search of his dad. "We opened it. In it she said she wanted to send him some letters and papers that had come for him after he left her house so she wanted to know whether he was at home to receive them if she sent them there. She said, too, that she hoped he was not offended by her not marrying him."

Wily Belle alluded to the older Budsberg going out west to homestead and so his family searched out there trying to find him, but of course they didn't as he was buried at Belle's. Their father had also borrowed money from a bank in Iola and when the note came due, the bank looked for him as well, and there's nothing more thorough then a bank looking to get its money back. They contacted Belle who told another story. Budsberg had been robbed in Chicago of most of his money and some clothes and had told her he would go out west and earn more money before any of his relatives learned about his loss. All of this didn't make sense to the young Budsberg who said his father had planned on staying in La Porte and had even ordered and sent seed potatoes to plant there.

This afternoon I viewed in the carriage house on the Gunness place, the remains of an unidentified man. I think they were the remains of my father but I would not swear to it. The size and shape of the head are the same as size and shape of my father's head. The mustache is like my father's which curled down over the mouth. Teeth are, I should think, like my father's, but I am not sure. These are the only points upon which I base the statement that I think the body is that of my father, Ole. O. Budsberg.

CORONER'S INQUISITION

Lucy Bergiat Sorenson

La Porte County Historical Society Archives

The subject of this inquest was found in the ruins of a burned residence on the farm of one Belle Gunness in LaPorte County, Indiana. The body was found by A. F. Smutzer and helpers on April 28, 1908 and is that of a white female child. No particular and minute description of this person can be given, owing to the fact that when found the body was partially incinerated. Distal end of each upper extremity was gone. Distal end of each lower extremities was gone. Further description of the body will be found in the depositions of Dr. Long. (Chas. S. Mack, Coroner)

DEPOSITION OF WITNESSES

Exhibit "G"

April 1908

La Porte County Historical Society Archives

Deposition taken 12th day of May, 1908, at Cutler's Morgue in LaPorte, Indiana over the dead body of unknown who was supposed to have come to her death by unknown cause.

Dr. H.H. Long being duly sworn deposes as follows:

"That he examined the corpse of a female which from appearances was about seven years of age.

"Externally the body showed evidence of having been severely burned. Flesh was black, charred in places and burned away as follows: In general body was most burned on anterior surfaces. Frontal bone of head was burned through exposing brain. . . .

"Both feet were off above the ankle and showed a burned stump. . . .

"Brain was examined showing no evidence of contusion or hemorrhage. What remained of skull showed no fracture."

CORONER'S INQUEST

Exhibit "A"

April 1908

La Porte County Historical Society Archives

The subject of this inquest was exhumed on the farm of one Belle Gunness in LaPorte County, Indiana. The body was found by A. F. Smutzer on May 6, 1908 and is that of an adult whose sex and color cannot be determined. Bones only of this body are left: no flesh adheres to them.

This was the only body found in this grave. It is the third grave opened by A. F. Smutzer on the farm of Belle Gunness. This grave lies between two graves opened by A. F. Smutzer on this farm yesterday.

And so it went. The transcript of the Coroner's Inquisition is fifty-seven pages and recounts, in the most scientific way, macabre finds, autopsies, and witness testimonies, including those who came searching for a loved one who had contact with Gunness.

The Cutler Funeral Home, still in business more than a century later, provided the difficult service of transporting body parts, and they allowed autopsies to be performed on site. And when it came time to bury the dead whose bodies hadn't been claimed and shipped back home, they provided those services too.

"White horses were used to haul women and children," says Richter. "Black horse pulled the hearse for the men."

BELLE'S STORY

Not pretty by any stretch of the imagination, Brynhild Paulsdatter Strseth, born in Selbu, Norway, in 1858, was a powerful woman standing over six feet tall and weighing more than two hundred eight pounds. And she seems to have had a personality to match.

Lured to Death by Love Letters

Mrs. Gunness' Victims Trapped by Her Craftiness

Washington Herald (**Washington, DC**), **Sunday, May 10, 1908**

Most of her acquaintances describe her as repulsive. Some of her neighbors go further. "More a devil than a woman," was the way William Desslelen put it, and he ought to know, because his farm is next to the Gunness place.

Cordial at First Only

"My aunt was always a strange woman," her nephew John Lawson, told the police the other day. "When you first knew her she would be very cordial. Then she was get offish.

She was always offish, to say the least, in LaPorte.

Growing up in an impoverished family, Belle, as she became known as the name was easily pronounced as well as connoting a delicate femininity, immigrated to the United States in 1881. Three years later, she married her first husband Mads Ditlev Anton Sorenson in Chicago, and the couple opened a confectionary store. Business wasn't good, but a mysterious fire that destroyed both their home and business proved to be much more profitable. The Sorensons collected the insurance money and suddenly Belle had a working business model.

Unfortunately for Mads, he didn't live long enough to enjoy the insurance money as he suddenly took ill and died within the very small window of time when both his old and new insurance policies overlapped. The doctor who arrived at the Sorensons' home thought he suffered from strychnine poisoning and suggested an autopsy. However, the grieving widow was so distraught at the thought of her dear husband being cut open and made such a fuss, that the doctor gave in. Besides, she said, Mads had an enlarged heart. Never mind that she had administered powders right before his death, she convinced the physician to list his death as due to a heart condition. In

The home of Belle Gunness and her first (or was it her second?) husband in Chicago where she most likely embarked on her business of murder for insurance money and as host for disposing of unwanted bodies. Photo courtesy of the La Porte County Historical Society.

cases like these, there always seems to be pesky relatives, and Mads's relations asked the police to investigate. It's not known if his body was exhumed but no charges were filed against Belle.

Mads was buried and his wife filed to collect the money on his insurance, the total sum was said to be around $8,500 or approximately $226,000 in today's dollars. The amount is even more impressive when you consider, according to barefootsworld.net, the average wage in 1908 was 22 cents per hour and the average worker made between $200 and $400 per year. Of course, professionals made more—accountants could expect to earn $2,000 per year, dentists $2,500, vets between $1,500 and $4,000, and a mechanical engineer about $5,000. In other words, Belle, an uneducated, most likely illiterate woman, made more than a highly trained, college-educated, engineer. And that engineer would have to work for a year to earn that amount, while Belle could kill many more people than that annually.

Belle and Mads supposedly had four children (some say they were childless), Caroline, Axel, Myrtle, and Lucy. Research on Find-A-Grave shows Axel Sorenson, the son of Belle and Mads, died in 1898, with the unusual notation (for this database) of, "Allegedly died of acute colitis like Caroline but symptoms were similar to those of many different types of poison. Life was insured and the life insurance company paid." Carolyn had died two years previously, also of acute colitis and also with the same notation. Both are said to be buried in Forest Hill Cemetery in Forest Hill, Illinois. The 1900 census lists two other children belonging to the couple—Myrtle and Lucy whose bodies would be identified in the remains of the 1908 fire. Also living with Belle at the time was a ten-year-old girl named Jennie Olsen.

Maybe Chicago was getting too hot for Belle, because in 1901, she used the insurance money to buy a farm in La Porte and moved there with her surviving children. A year later, on April 1, 1902, she married either her second or third husband, a widower named Peter Gunness (she might have married in Norway before moving to the United States).

Peter had two children. An infant daughter died a week after the marriage. She, unfortunately, had been left alone in the house with Belle on the day she died. Before the end of the year, the happy groom would be dead as well, supposedly scalded by hot brine while reaching for his slippers and then clobbered over the head by a heavy meat grinder that somehow tipped over from a top shelf.

Peter's other daughter, Swanhild, was fortunately scooped up by his brother Gust and taken to live with his family in Wisconsin. Of all the children in Belle's orbit, she was the only one to survive.

With Peter in the ground, Gunness began running personal ads in both English and Scandinavian newspapers throughout the Midwest. Though each was designed for lonely men who wanted both companionship and financial comfort, the ads varied somewhat.

"Widow, with mortgaged farm, seeks marriage. Triflers need not apply."

Another ad, written by a neighbor, which ran in the Chicago papers, said: "A rich and good-looking woman, the owner of a big farm, desires to correspond with a gentleman of wealth and refinement. Object, matrimony. Scandinavian preferred."

Bingo for Belle! Postmaster Small testified in court that Belle was getting four to ten letters a day. These came from everywhere but particularly from the Northwest.

It got to be a joke around the Post Office," said Small about the flood of mail, for the advertiser was anything but a comely woman. Indeed, contemporary accounts describe her as fat and unkempt with unattractive features. But the letters came fast and thick and neighbors began to notice strange men arriving at the Gunness farm."

What these men thought when first seeing Belle is unknown. Her farmhouse was a true "Hotel California," a classic rock song by the Eagles whose ending lyrics are: "You can check-out any time you like, but you can never leave."

In 1908, when the story broke, La Porte was a small farming community located in Northwest Indiana with a population of about 10,500. But the grisly murder scene and a suspect termed as a "Female Blue Beard" attracted even the sustained interest of the venerable *New York Times,* which ran numerous articles about the Belle and her hapless suitors.

Reading a letter written in reply to a man answering her advertisement shows an amazingly strong marketing skill on her part.

WELCOME TO MY PARLOR SAID THE SPIDER TO THE FLY

Letter from Mrs. Gunness

New York Times, **Friday, May 8, 1908**

The letter which Carl Petersen of Waupaca received from Mrs. Belle Gunness, the alleged LaPorte murderess, has been translated from Norwegian into English. It says in part:

"Carl Petersen, Waupaca, Wis:

Dear Sir: As some time ago I received from you a letter in answer to my ad in the *Scandinavian*, I will with pleasure answer the same.

The reason I waited for some time is that there has been other answers to the ad. As many as fifty have been received and it has been impossible to answer all. I have picked out the most respectable and I have decided that yours is such.

First, I will tell you that I am a Norwegian and have been in this country for twenty years. I live in Indiana, about 59 miles from Chicago and one-mile north of LaPorte. I am the sole owner of a nice home, pretty location.

There are 75 acres of land, also all kinds of crops, improved land, apples, plums and currants. Am on a boulevard road and have a 12-room house, practically new, a windmill and all modern improvements, situated in a beautiful suburb of Chicago, worth about $15,000.

All of these is pretty near paid for. It is in my own name. I am alone with three small children, from 5 to 11 years old. The smallest is a boy. The largest are girls, all frisky and well. I lost my husband by accident five years ago and have since tried to get along as well as I could with what help I could hire. I am getting tired of this and I found that it is not well to trust others with so much.

Now if you think that you are able in some way to put up $1000 cash we can talk matters over personally. If you cannot, is it worthwhile to consider. I would not care for you as a hired hand as I am tired of that and need a little rest in my home and near my children. I will close for this time."

The letter is signed Mrs. P.S. Gunness, LaPorte, Ind.

The day before the fire, according to the *New York Daily News* on November 30, 2014, she had visited an attorney in La Porte to draft a will in order "to prepare for an eventuality. I'm afraid that fool Lamphere is going to kill me and burn my house."

Talk about setting the stage.

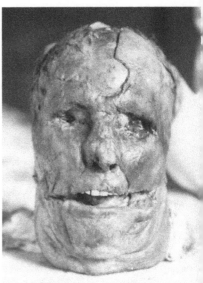

Andrew Helgelien, before and after meeting Belle. Photos courtesy of the La Porte County Historical Society.

Before returning home, she bought a few items including toys, cream puffs, and a five-gallon can of gasoline.

Questioned after the fire and the bodies were found, Lamphere told the police, "After all, she wanted me killed because I knew too much."

In the photo of him on display at the museum, Andrew Helgelien, while not movie star handsome, looks presentable. Dressed in a starched white shirt with tie and suit coat, his hair patented down, he looks out into the camera showing a serious face with hopeful eyes. It is hoped he wasn't seeing his future.

Andrew had responded to an ad placed by Belle in the *Scandinavian* that read: "Wanted—a woman who owns a beautifully located and valuable farm in first class condition, wants a good and reliable man as partner in the same." When Helgelien responded to her ad, Belle wrote back a letter welcoming him into her life if he would help pay off the farm's mortgage, ending the letter with "My

Asle Helgelien, worried about his brother Andrew, traveled to La Porte and helped identify the body. Photo courtesy of the La Porte County Historical Society.

heart beats wild rapture for you. My Andrew, I love you. Come prepared to stay forever."

Gunness certainly ensured that last sentence was true.

Andrew arrived at Belle's with $3,000, and his family never heard from him again. Worried, Asle Helgelien, Andrew's brother, contacted Gunness who said he'd left for Norway. Reading about the fire, Asle next contacted the Indiana State Police, saying he believed that Belle had murdered his brother and set the fire as a cover-up. The police were less than impressed with this, but Asle was determined. He came to La Porte with a letter written by Belle to Andrew.

> To the Dearest Friend in the World: No woman in the world is happier than I am. I know that you are now to come to me and be my own. I can tell from your letters that you are the man I want. It does not take one long to tell when to like a person, and you I like better than anyone in the world, I know. Think how we will enjoy each other's company. You, the sweetest man in the whole world. We will be all alone with each other. Can you conceive of anything

Digging for bodies following the fire at Gunness farm on April 8, 1908. Photo courtesy of the La Porte County Historical Society.

nicer? I think of you constantly. When I hear your name mentioned, and this is when one of the dear children speaks of you, or I hear myself humming it with the words of an old love song, it is beautiful music to my ears.

My heart beats in wild rapture for you, My Andrew, I love you. Come prepared to stay forever.

Taking Care of Business, Belle-Style

Belle may have expanded her business model further. As police kept digging, and digging, they began to turn up female skeletons and paraphernalia that didn't belong to her children. On May 22, it was reported by the *New York Times* that jewelry belonging to May O'Reilly, who lived in Troup Street, Rochester, New York, was found by Sheriff Smultzer, who communicated the fact to the Rochester police. They replied by telegram that O'Reilly had disappeared from her home several months ago. With incidents like these and the trunks arriving from Chicago, thought to carry human remains, there was speculation Belle was also running a burial service for others who had their own murder rackets going on.

Considering her ability to lure hapless men to give her money and the probability that she was accepting, and burying, bodies from other murderers, Belle apparently possessed good managerial skills and knew how to successfully grow her business, branching out into other related areas.

The *New York Times* agreed. As a May 7, 1908 article put it:

The presence of women among the victims of the murder mill and the fact that one of them at least was dismembered before being deposited in the ground leads to partial confirmation of the theory that Mrs. Gunness was running a murder fence as well as being in the business herself and that some of the murders, especially those of the women were committed in Chicago and the bodies shipped to her to be disposed of.

This theory again is strengthening by the additional fact that gunny sacks or pieces of decayed gunny sacks were found in the graves, and in all such cases the bodies had been dismembered. To place the bodies in sacks for shipment in trunks would be a very natural thing and to the police it does not seem possible that Mrs. Gunness would have the sacks on hand or would have purchased them for such a purpose.

In the case of some of the victims the reverse was true, two skeletons were found upon a piece of old mattress and another had been burned in a nude state, and in neither case was the victim's body dismembered.

BELIEVES MISS OLSEN SLAIN

Girl's Sweetheart Tells of Her Disappearance from Gunness Farm

New York Times, **Sunday, May 10, 1908**

Special to the *New York Times*. OKLAHOMA CITY, Oklahoma, May 9— Emil Greening of Oklahoma City, the sweetheart of Jennie Olsen, who is believed to have been killed by Mrs. Belle Gunness, worked for the woman as a farm hand last summer, coming to Oklahoma a few months ago. He was found today with his brother Fred, who also worked for Mrs. Gunness. He told of a dozen or more men who had visited the woman and mysteriously disappeared.

"Jennie and I were good friends," said Greening today, "and when Mrs. Gunness planned to send her to California she came to me and told me she would never go. I was away on an errand the next afternoon and when I returned I was told that Jennie and a professor, who came after her, had gone.

I wrote to her several times and gave the letters to Mrs. Gunness to mail but never received an answer."

Greening is satisfied that the Olsen girl was murdered but declared that her body had not yet been found.

A conspirator later detailed Ms. Gunness's favorite method for murder: a little chloroform in a tumbler of whiskey, followed by a strychnine chaser. Once her gentleman callers dropped dead, she would wait for dark to dismember and bury the bodies.

Why would anyone kill so many people particularly those she had raised and cared for such as her children and stepchildren? There were plenty of theories.

INDIANA MURDERS LAID TO FANATIC

Theory Advanced That Mrs. Gunness Was Led into Crime by Sudden Wealth

———————

Trail Widow in Illinois

———————

*Police to Dig Up Yard of Her Austin Home—
Girl Friend of Lamphere Arrested*

New York Times, **Friday, May 8, 1908**

"Mrs. Belle Gunness was a religious fanatic, self-hypnotized into crime"—this was the solution of the LaPorte horror, so far as motive is concerned, offered by Dr. Charles E. Jones of Austin to-day.

MRS. GUNNESS WAS MONEY MAD

Sister Says Her Weakness Was Greed—
May Exhume Husband's Body

Special to the *New York Times*, Thursday, May 7, 1908

Chicago, May 6—The next step in the LaPorte murder mystery is to be a police investigation to discover whether or not Mrs. Belle Gunness conducted a private graveyard in Chicago before removing to LaPorte.

The body of her former husbands may be exhumed for examination but the Coroner has not fully decided upon this step. Her first husband, Mads Sorenson, died suddenly and under peculiar circumstances at 621 Alma Street. He had $4000 insurance on his life which his widow collected and then moved to Michigan. Then she married Gunness and settled on a farm in LaPorte. Gunness, too, died suddenly. He had $3500 insurance on his life.

"My sister was crazy for money," declared Mrs. Nellie Larson of 992 North Francisco Avenue, who is Mrs. Gunness's sister. "That was her great weakness. As a young woman she never seemed to care for a man for his own self, only for the money or luxury he was able to give her.

"When living with her first husband in Austin she used to say, 'I would never remain with this man if it was not for the nice home he has.'"

The Gunness woman's trail was followed in Chicago by investigators who traced her history back to the time she moved to Austin, nearly 28 years ago. The addresses at which she lived were:

Grand Avenue and North Forty-third Avenue. Frame cottage.

Elizabeth and Grand Avenue. Ran a grocery and notion store.

621 Alma Street.

Austin Avenue and Sophia Street.

Two of the houses were burned and the woman collected insurance.

Revelations of the day developed that besides her first husband, the burial lot in Forest Home contains the bodies of two children supposed to have been hers. The record of the deaths of these children is being investigated.

Neighbors crowded about the number in Alma Street, half a block from West Chicago Avenue, expecting the digging for bodies would begin in the rear yard.

Coroner Hoffman said he would commence at once whatever search might be necessary in Chicago to unravel the tragic deeds of Mrs. Gunness's life.

4 MORE SKELETONS IN INDIANA MYSTERY

Police Believe Some Were Shipped from Chicago in Trunks to Mrs. Gunness's Farm. Widow May Not Be Dead

———————

Search Is Being Made for Woman Who Advertised for Husbands—Two Women among Victims

Special to the *New York Times*, Thursday, May 7, 1908

The record of Mrs. Belle Gunness as a dealer in assassination was enhanced greatly to-day by the discovery of four more skeletons in the yard and barn lot of her late residence, and it is more than probable that the number of murders will reach a score or more before the burying ground at the widow's home is depopulated of her victims.

Testimony of drayman who had carted trunks and boxes to the Gunness home lent color to the supposition that the bodies had been shipped to Mrs. Gunness . . . the victims had been dismembered and in this grave was also found pieces of gunny sacks.

Not a thing was found by which any of the bodies could be identified. A heavy red mustache was found in one of the graves and it is believed it was once worn by a North Dakota ranchman who came to see Mrs. Gunness in answer to her matrimonial advertisements. He professed a willingness to marry her, but insisted that she accompany him to his Western home. This she refused to and he later disappeared. She gave out that the engagement had been broken off because she would not go to North Dakota to live and that the ranchman had returned home. Nothing has been heard from him since and the authorities are trying to discover if he can be accounted for.

CLUE TO MRS. GUNNESS

Two Young Women Tell Detroit Police LaPorte Widow Is Alive

New York Times, **Sunday, June 28, 1908**

The Detroit police believe they are on the trail of Mrs. Belle Gunness of LaPorte, Ind., who is suspected of wholesale murders on her farm near that city. Two young women whom the police had in custody yesterday afternoon and evening are said to have met Mrs. Gunness since her supposed burned body was found in the ruins of her home.

The police assert that the statements of the two young women convinced them that Mrs. Gunness is still alive. They gave the names of other persons who are also said to know that the woman is alive and the police are looking for them.

MRS. GUNNESS IN MEXICO?

Ambassador Thompson Tells of Suspected Assassin in Masculine Attire

New York Times, **Sunday, June 14, 1908**

It is suggested by a dispatch received at the State Department today from Ambassador Thompson at Mexico City, that Mrs. Belle Gunness, on whose farm in Indiana many bodies of murdered persons were found, may be in Mexico. The dispatch says the woman discovered answers the description of the Indiana assassin.

Ambassador Thompson says he received the information through the Governor of Chiapas, as follows:

"A few days ago an American woman about 50 years old, five feet seven inches in height, dark blue eyes, light chestnut hair, slightly gray, quick nervous step, passed by Palenque. Was traveling alone and without baggage and has no letters of recommendations. Left Salt de Aqua wearing masculine clothing of khaki. Made inquiries of communication with Usumacinta River and plunged into the interior alone, not heeding warnings as to danger. As she might be American female assassin Gunness, give you these details and await instructions."

No instructions have been sent to Ambassador Thompson, the information being too indefinite to warrant positive action.

SAW MRS. GUNNESS ALIVE

New York Times, **Sunday, November 22, 1908**

The testimony of three witnesses who declared that they saw Mrs. Belle Gunness alive several months after the fire that destroyed her home constituted the most interesting development in the trial to-day of Ray Lamphere.

LAMPHERE GUILTY, ARSON, NOT MURDER

Farmhand Convicted of Burning House, but Not of Killing Mrs. Gunness and Children

———————

Jury Explains Verdict

———————

Satisfied Body in Ruins Was Widow's, but Decided Case on a Different Proposition—Sentenced to Prison

New York Times, **Friday, November 27, 1908**

Ray Lamphere, charged with arson and the murder of Mrs. Belle Gunness and her three children by setting fire to the Gunness house on April 28, was this evening found guilty of arson by the jury which had the case under consideration for twenty-four hours. On November 26, 1908, he was sentenced to 20 years at the state prison in Michigan City.

By December of the following year, he was dead of tuberculosis. But Lamphere had confessed to being Belle's accomplice and setting the fire, and he said Belle was still alive.

A photo of him in jail shows a large bouquet of flowers behind him. Richter believes that's proof he and Belle were still in collusion. "Where else would he get the flowers?" she asks. It is indeed a good question.

Several people involved with the investigation would later take the Belle show on the road, hosting crowds to see the grisly memorabilia at her barn and traveling around the state showing it off. It proved to be a money-making attraction.

Asle K. Hegelien was able to identify his brother Andrew who was the last man standing, so to speak in that house of horrors known as the Gunness farm. Andrew was more easily recognizable (though he wasn't in the greatest of shape) because of that.

Buried at the Patton Cemetery in La Porte, Andrew's tombstone reads: "Andrew Hegelien, 1859–1908. The Last Victim of the Gunness Horror. Remains Found by His Brother Asle K. Hegelien, May 5, 1908. Rest in Peace."

As for Belle, the last sighting took place in 1931. After that no one saw her again. Well, at least in the flesh. Richter shows me a photo snapped near the shed from her farm that was dissembled and then put back together as part of the exhibit.

"Look at this," she says, pointing a person standing. Indeed, next to the unsuspecting museum visitor I can see the hazy outline of what looks to be a large woman.

Richter who seems very much like a no-nonsense historian and researcher, says that those who work in the museum often feel as though Belle is with them, particularly in the area where the artifacts from her life, her farm, and her victims on our display. Which makes sense. Since she burned down her farm, where else would she go?

9

Bootlegging, Missing Wills, Disappearing Jewels, Deadly Encounters: The Story of Nettie and Harry Diamond

RICH WIFE, DYING, RALLIES TO PIN PLOT ON SPOUSE;
SAYS BOY HUSBAND SHOT HER AND CHAUFFEUR

Mrs. Diamond Spurned Judas Kill of Harry after He Shot Her

Chicago Daily Tribune, **February 16, 1923**

What I know about an Indiana murder.

I lived around the corner from where Nettie Diamond spent her last night before her husband Harry shot her. My fourth-grade teacher's grandmother was Anna Cohen Fishman, Nettie's best friend, the one who was with her when she lay dying in the hospital after being shot at close range (the four bullets were still in her gut) and being savagely beaten (there were fourteen blows) around the head with the end of a revolver. When I was twelve, I spent my Christmas vacation addressing envelopes for Lloyd Hurst, Nettie's son, an attorney, restaurateur, and insurance agent. On my way to the movie theater, I would pass by the drugstores that she and Sam had owned (Nettie was a pharmacist who graduated from Columbia University in 1904). Bernie Hurst, Nettie's son with her second husband, Dr. Samuel Herskovitz, was my elementary school principal.

But I didn't know any of this until, when my mother was ninety-two, she told me she'd dated Mr. Hurst when both attended Indiana University. He'd given her a ring, she said, but then decided they couldn't marry as she wasn't Jewish. She married my father who became the superintendent of East Chicago Public Schools. In other words, he was Bernie's boss.

But Bernie's last name wasn't really Hurst, my mother told me. It was Herskovitz or Hurshwitz or something like that. They changed the name because his mother had been murdered out by the old Palm Grove restaurant, the one with the pink and green neon sign in, you got it, the shape of a palm tree. We'd go there when I was a child, sitting in one of the pink banquettes and I would order my favorite, the Chicago classic Shrimp de Jonghe. I didn't know then that right there fifty years earlier, on Valentine's Day 1923, Harry had shot Nettie in the backseat of their chauffeur-driven car and then tried to shoot the chauffeur as he ran away. The Palm Grove hadn't even been built yet. The land was still raw prairie and the road little better than gravel. It was a short cut, Harry had said, as they went to the bank to cash the $15,000 check Nettie had in her purse from the sale of stock. She also had four big diamonds and about $500 in cash. Nettie had money and she was getting tired of Harry and all his women and all his mooching.

She was tired of his roadhouse, The Berghoff Inn, just on the other side of Gary where he did the books, supplied the bootlegged booze, and dated the girls who went with men for money. She was tired of his antics, such as him giving an expensive dress to their twenty-year-old maid, the one she had fired. If she knew about it, she sure would have been tired of him flirting with her thirteen-year-old daughter, the music genius, A-student, pretty as a picture, Pearl. And Pearl was certainly tired of creepy Harry.

Harry knew he was on his way out as far as Nettie was concerned, and worse, she was going to change her will. So he tried to set it up so she was dead and Armstrong, the kid chauffeur he'd hired the previous week, would be dead too. But Armstrong fought him off and got away, and a passing truck picked up the fleeing eighteen-year-old who was shouting "murder."

Nettie played dead all the way to the drugstore as Harry drove, but as soon as he dumped her body on the ground, there in her mink coat with its four bloody bullet holes, she opened her eyes and said to everyone in the room, "You killed me Harry."

He kept saying no, it was the "colored" guy, the chauffeur. But Nettie was having none of that. Witnesses in the drugstore later testified that she said, "You shot me yourself" and "The Negro didn't shoot me." Frankie Simbolos, the guy from the gas station next door; Hershel Cannon, the pharmacist; Koochis, the railroad guy just off from work; Storer the clerk; and everyone else who had stopped by to see what was going on because of the brand new Hudson sedan out front with its door open and gun on the front seat, all told the police and then the jury that Nettie had announced, "He has $20,000 of my money and that is the reason he shot me." She didn't stop saying it, not when Townsley showed up nor when the police did. They put her on a stretcher and in an ambulance and took her to the nearest hospital then—the one in Gary run by nuns (most hospitals in Lake County, Indiana, were run by nuns back then.

Nettie was too tough to die, despite the wounds that the doctors, including her good friend Frank Townsley, examined but were unable to treat. Frank was the first to arrive at the drugstore that Nettie owned, which was where Harry had taken her after she played dead.

They took Harry to the police station where he says they beat him, but if they did he sure deserved it.

"I could hardly recognize her as a human being," Storer, the clerk testified in court, "Her face and head appeared to be a mass of matter; it didn't look like a face of an individual at all. Dr. Townsley said to me they were bad wounds."

Harry had done this to her because she didn't want him anymore, and he still wanted her money.

As Harry was heading east to the jail in the East Chicago City Hall, the police paddy wagon passed the telephone office where the truck driver had taken Armstrong. Inside Armstrong was being treated for his wounds and telling the police the same story Nettie was telling down at the drugstore. Tough luck, Harry. Armstrong at least would live about fifty years or so. His only daughter would grow up to be a teacher and impact many children's lives—all because he got away. Good job, William.

Townsley and the surgeon who operated on her later that afternoon said they didn't know how she lived so long, how she stayed conscious so long and kept talking and talking about what Harry had done.

But I know how because I read all the newspaper articles, it was a big story back then, and I read the State Supreme Court transcript when Harry appealed his guilty verdict (it didn't work and they electrocuted him in November 1924—the first and only Jew to be executed in Indiana—nice distinction, Harry). I read her divorce papers from previous marriages, her lawsuits (Nettie liked to sue), and her real estate dealings. I read all I could find and then I looked for more. I researched because Nettie was the mother of the man my mother had wanted to marry and besides, her story was so fascinating.

I read so much that I knew more about Nettie than her grandkids did. She married Louis Zauderer in New York when she was still in pharmacy school and he had just graduated. They moved to St. Louis and he owned a couple of pharmacies and gave her one as a birthday present. Then she divorced him because she wanted to marry Sam who was also originally from Romania and had just graduated from George Washington University's medical school in St. Louis. Sam was a little bit of a grifter too. Handsome and splendid, he had lived platonically (or so they say) with a married woman who paid his tuition and room and board. When left her, she was mad and told her story to the newspaper and tried to sue him but it didn't matter because Sam wanted Nettie.

Louis didn't show up in court, and Nettie got custody of Edward, their five-year-old-son. But she left him in St. Louis to move to Indiana Harbor, my hometown, with Sam.

Nettie Sachs Herskovitz, in white, standing by the prescription counter in one of the drugstores she and her husband, Dr. Samuel Herskovitz, owned. Photo courtesy of the East Chicago Public Library.

My grandparents on my father's side were from Romania too, and they lived just down the block from Sam's office and Nettie's pharmacy. I imagine they took their kids to Dr. Herskovitz because he spoke their language. That means that my dad and my Aunt Mary and Uncles Charles and John probably knew Sam until he died of some stomach problem in 1916. And no, I don't think it was murder despite the snide remarks of my friends who mention Nettie's knowledge of pharmacology. Sam and Nettie's first child, Pearl, was born in 1909 and then quickly there were Bernard, Lloyd, and Cecil, and then Sam was gone.

Two years later, Nettie married Sol, a Chicago doctor also from Romania, but they divorced just three months later after Sol claimed she tried to kill him and Nettie admitted it in court. "I'd do it again," she told the judge and they wrote it down in the divorce proceedings in that fancy handwriting they used back then and which is so hard to read just like she said it. It was when she was divorcing Dr. Golden that I found out Nettie went by Nellie too. Nettie still has secrets I haven't found yet. But they're getting fewer.

So she was free again and then she met Harry. He was fourteen, sixteen, or even twenty years younger. It's hard to say because no one really knows how old Nettie was. Somewhere between thirty-three and forty-two—even her death certificate is different from her tombstone—and forget figuring out the census counts. She was always twenty-one or twenty-nine. Louis said she was fifteen when they married in 1902. But really, she was in pharmacy school. At fifteen? Well, maybe. She was terrifically smart. Except about Harry.

Any woman who wasn't crazy in love could tell that Harry was bad news. Good looking even in his death row pictures, just one look tells you all you need to know. He'd break your heart and lie and cheat and steal from you while all the time telling you how crazy he was about you and some babe, younger, prettier, would be outside sitting in the car waiting for him. He was that type.

Nettie kept putting up bail because he got caught stealing barrels of liquor or driving too fast or doing something he shouldn't have. But then maybe Nettie wasn't so clean either. She and Harry were probably fencing diamonds with some guys in Chicago; she knew about his bootlegging and pouring bad booze into good bottles; and they also got in trouble for trying to get someone to commit perjury so she could break the lease on her drugstore. The drugstore where Harry brought her body. It was lucky for Nettie that Herschel Cannon was still willing to call the police because he must have been sore.

At the hospital, Anna told Nettie she needed to change her will and so she did, calling her lawyer to come over right now. She didn't have a lot of time. She held on until the next morning when the police came and she gave them her statement. Gave it right to Harry too. I wonder if he felt it all those miles away in the East Chicago hooch-gow (that's what they called jail back then).

Nettie was so weak at first she could only make an "x."

But when the police chief suggested she'd better sign her name, that the court might want her signature, she raised herself up high enough to sign a frail Nettie D. Diamond. If you knew Nettie, then you knew she would do what it takes. She was the woman who graduated from Columbia at a time when most women didn't go to college. She was the woman who was only one of seven women out of eight hundred or so men who graduated that year from pharmacy school. And she may have been only fifteen. That's Nettie.

Exhausted after signing her name, she laid back down.

She turned to Anna, my fourth-grade teacher's grandmother, the one I lived just around the corner from, and she said, "Anna, I can't fight anymore." Everyone in the room heard it. And then she closed her eyes, and Nettie died.

But not before she sent Harry to the chair.

10

The Lady and the Dragon: How Madge Oberholtzer Brought Down the KKK

STEPHENSON HELD FOR DEATH OF GIRL

*Indiana Officials Accuse Ex-Ku Klux Dragon
and Two Others of Attack on Her*

THEY ARE REFUSED BAIL

*Missing Suspects in the Oberholtzer Case Were Found
in the Office of Their Attorney*

New York Times, **Tuesday, April 21, 1925**

D. C. Stephenson, ex-Grand Dragon of the Ku Klux Klan in Indiana, along with Earl Klnck and Earl Gentry, who were indicted on Saturday by the Marion County Grand Jury on a charge of murder in the first degree, growing out of the death of Miss Madge Oberholtzer of this city, are locked behind iron bars tonight after their two-day flight.

Despite her screams of terror and pain and their assertion of being the protectors of womanhood, none of Klansmen aboard the train traveling from Indianapolis to Hammond went to the aid of

Madge Augustine Oberholtzer as she was brutalized and raped by Davis Curtis Stephenson, Grand Dragon of the KKK in twenty-three Northern states.

The year was 1925 and Indiana's Klan membership was at its zenith with 350,000, a number that included not only 30 percent of the white male population but also members of the Women's Ku Klux Klan (WKKK). Indeed, Indiana had one of the largest Klan presences in the United States. The *Fiery Cross,* a weekly Klan newspaper published in Indianapolis beginning with the July 20, 1922 issue and ceasing in February 1925, featured such headlines as "Protestant Ticket Sweeps State: National Papal Machine Smashed" and "Roman Thugs Attack Law-Abiding Citizens." There was railing against newspapers such as the *Indianapolis Times* that were viewed as propaganda tools for Catholics seeking to lie to the public.

Then as now, there were those evil immigrants who were murdering Americans as evidenced in this *Fiery Cross* headline "Foreigners Kill Two Klansmen and Wound Many Americans."

There was even a Junior Klan since it's never too early to teach hatred.

When Stephenson, who had his headquarters in a lavish mansion in Indianapolis, stated "I am the law," it wasn't an empty boast. He was the mastermind behind the election of fellow Klansman Governor Edward Jackson and a large contingent of state legislators who were also members of the Klan. His behind-the-scenes power enabled him to amass a fortune and develop such a sense of power that he kept a bust of Napoleon on his desk, seeing similarities between the emperor of France and himself.

A showman, Stephenson flew to rallies, landing in front of the large crowds (20,000 showed up in 1923 in Valparaiso to see him and at another rally, Klansmen from neighboring states as well as Indiana swelled the Kokomo gathering to 200,000). To these adoring crowds, he'd deliver his hateful diatribes before being whisked away in a white automobile. He knew how to work a crowd.

His dream was to become a U.S. senator.

But that was before Oberholtzer, who had disappeared for two days, was delivered to her parents' home with chunks of her flesh bitten out of her bruised and battered body. Emotionally fraught by what she had endured, Oberholtzer had taken a dose of bichloride of mercury and was in agony as the chemical burned through her body.

THE DYING DECLARATION OF MADGE OBERHOLTZER: THE KEY EVIDENCE IN THE 1925 TRIAL OF D. C. STEPHENSON

Liebowitz, *My Indiana*, 1964

I, Madge Oberholtzer, being in full possession of my mental faculties and conscious that I am about to die, make as my dying declaration the following statements: My name is Madge Oberholtzer. I am a resident of Marion County, State of Indiana, residing at No. 5802 University Avenue, Indianapolis. I first met D. C. Stephenson at the banquet given for the Governor at the Athletic Club early in January, 1925.

After the banquet he asked me for a date several times, but I gave him no definite answer. He later insisted that I take dinner with him at the Washington Hotel and I consented and he came for me at my home in his Cadillac car, and on this occasion we dined together. After that he called me several times on the phone, and once again I had dinner with him at the Washington Hotel with another party.

Invited to a party at Stephenson's home where several prominent people were in attendance, Oberholtzer saw the Grand Dragon again on March 15, 1925. When she returned home about ten o'clock in the evening, her mother told her she'd had several calls and was to call Irvington 0492. "I called Irvington 0492 and Stephenson answered and said to me to come down if I could to his home that he wished to see me about something very important to me; that he was leaving for Chicago and had to see me before he left. His home was only two or three blocks from mine," she said in her statement.

Stephenson said he was too busy and couldn't leave his house, so instead he sent a Mr. Gentry whom Madge had never met before. Together they walked to Stephenson's home. As soon as she entered the house, Madge could see that Stephenson had been drinking heavily. Also in the room was Stephenson's chauffeur, a young man nicknamed Shorty; Earl Klinck joined them as well.

This wasn't a situation the young and naïve Madge was used to and she told the police she was very afraid and became even more so when it became apparent she was the only woman in the house.

Leading her into the kitchen, the men tried to get her to drink. When she resisted, they forced her.

I was afraid not to do so and I drank three small glasses of the drink. This made me very ill and dazed and I vomited. Stephenson said to me about this time, "I want you to go with me to Chicago." I remember saying I could not and would not. I was very much terrified and did not know what to do. I said to him that I wanted to go home. He said, "No, you cannot go home. Oh, yes! You are going with me to Chicago. I love you more than any woman I have ever known." I tried to call my home on the phone but could get no answer. Later when I tried to get to a phone they would not let me.

These men were all about me. They took me up to Stephenson's room, and he opened a dresser drawer which was filled with revolvers. He told each of the men to take one, and he selected a pearl-handled revolver for himself and had Shorty load it. Stephenson said first to me that we were going to drive through to Chicago. He said for me to go with him, but I said I did not wish to and would not go to Chicago. Later Gentry called the Washington Hotel, at Stephenson's order, and secured reservation in a drawing room for two persons. They all took me to the automobile at the rear of Stephenson's yard and we started the trip.

I thought we were bound for Chicago but did not know. I begged of them to drive past my home so I could get my hat, and once inside my home I thought I would be safe from them. They drove me to Union Station in the machine, where they had to get a ticket. I did not get out of the automobile all the way.

As strange and terrifying as it all was, it was soon to become more evil and twisted for Oberholtzer who was kept inside of the car as the men made several stops. It's easy to envision her rising fear as Shorty drove the car through the dark and empty streets. She was, she said, afraid he'd kill her. She felt even more helpless hearing Stephenson boast to Gentry about how smart he was to have lured her into this trap.

At the station, there was no one to see them except a porter. Once aboard, Oberholtzer was taken to a compartment. She couldn't remember much of what happened next. Her memories were of Gentry climbing into the top berth while Stephenson took the hem of her dress and pulled it over her head.

I tried to fight but was weak and unsteady. Stephenson took hold of my two hands and held them. I had not the strength to move. What I had drunk was affecting me. Stephenson took all my clothes off and pushed me into the lower berth. After the train had started, Stephenson got in with me and attacked me. He held me so I could not move. I did not know and do not remember all that happened. He chewed me all over my body, bit my neck and face, chewing my tongue, chewed my breasts until they bled, my back, my legs, my ankles and mutilated me all over my body. I remember I heard a buzz early in the morning and the porter calling us to get up for Hammond and Gentry shook me and said it was time to get up that we were to get off at Hammond.

At this time I was becoming more conscious and Stephenson was flourishing his revolver. I said to him to shoot me. He held the revolver against my side, but I did not flinch. I said to him again to kill me, but he put the gun in his grip. I had heard no sound from Gentry during the night. Afterwards Gentry and

Stephenson helped me dress and the two men dressed and they took me off the train at Hammond. I remember seeing the conductor. I was able to walk to the Indiana Hotel. I remember begging Stephenson and saying to him to wire my mother during the night and he said he had or would, I am not clear about that. At the Indiana Hotel, Stephenson registered for himself and wife. I tried to see under what name but failed to do so.

It was about 6:30 in the morning when they all went up to Room 416. Madge had no money and kept begging Stephenson to send her mother a telegram. He promised he would and dictated what she should write. Then he fell asleep. Gentry put hot towels and hazel on her head and bathed her body to help with the pain. When Stephenson woke up, he somewhat apologized, saying he was sorry and that "was three degrees less than a brute" to which she responded "You are worse than that." " Breakfast was served. Stephenson consumed grapefruit, coffee, sausage, and buttered toast. As for Madge, she wasn't hungry and didn't eat, barely managing to sip some coffee.

Plotting to escape, she asked Stephenson for money to buy a hat, which he gave her. Shorty chauffeured her to a store near the hotel where she purchased a small black silk hat for $12.50. Returning to the Cadillac, she asked Shorty to take her to the drugstore as she wanted to buy rouge. Instead, Oberholtzer purchased a box of bichloride of mercury tablets which she put in her coat pocket.

Back at the hotel, Stephenson and the other men were drinking and making plans to go to Chicago. Gentry was in room 417, and Madge asked if she could rest there.

That wasn't part of Stephenson's game plan and he told her to lie down next to him. Waiting until he was asleep, Madge laid out eighteen of the bichloride of mercury tablets with the intent of taking them all but they burned so badly she managed to swallow only six. Oberholtzer continued in her dying declaration:

Earlier in the morning I had taken Stephenson's revolver, and while Gentry was out sending the telegram I wanted to kill myself then in Stephenson's presence. This was while he was first asleep. Then I decided to try and get poison and take it in order to save my mother from disgrace. I knew it would take longer with the mercury tablets to kill me. Later, after I had taken the mercury tablets, I lay down on the bed and became very ill. I think. It was nearly four o'clock in the afternoon before anyone came into the room where I was. Then Shorty came in. He sat down to talk to me.

Seeing she looked ill, Shorty asked what was wrong and at first she didn't respond. She was in intense pain, almost delirious, and had been vomiting blood most of the day so Shorty persisted.

"Where is your pain," Shorty wanted to know and she said all over.

When he responded that there couldn't be pain without cause, she asked if he could keep a secret and said she'd taken poison but not to tell Stephenson.

Shorty turned pale at her words and said he was going to take a walk. A few minutes later, he came back with Gentry and Stephenson. All three were upset. Stephenson ordered a quart of milk and when it arrived, made her drink it. Madge told him she'd taken the tables and added, "If you don't believe it there is evidence on the floor and in the cuspidor."

Stephenson emptied the cuspidor into the bathtub and saw it was half full of clotted blood.

Stephenson said he was going to take her to the hospital where she could register as his wife but Madge refused. He told her she could say she'd taken the mercury tablets by mistake thinking they were aspirin and they'd pump out her stomach. But she refused to register as his wife and so he said they'd take her home but she didn't want to do that either. She said she wanted to stay there and they should just leave and go about their business or let her register under her own name.

"We'll do nothing of the kind," Stephenson replied. "We will take you home."

But first he thought they should go to Crown Point and get married. Gentry was in agreement but again Madge refused. Snapping his fingers, Stephenson told Shorty to "pack the grips."

Stephenson helped her downstairs and just as they were leaving Hammond, she asked Shorty to call her mother.

"If I do that she will be right up here," was his reply.

"What could be sweeter?" asked Madge.

Stephenson replied that he'd already called her mother and had told her she wouldn't be coming home that night.

Madge, in excruciating pain, couldn't remember much of what happened after they put her in the back seat and drove southeast toward Indianapolis.

> After we got a piece Stephenson said to Shorty to take the auto license plates off of the car, which he did, and Stephenson said to him to say if questioned that we had parked in the last town we had passed through and auto plates had been stolen. All the way back to Indianapolis I suffered great pain and agony and screamed for a doctor. I said I wanted a hypodermic to ease the pain, but they refused to stop. I begged and said to Stephenson to leave me along the road some place that someone would stop and take care of me if he wouldn't. I said to him that I felt he was crueler to me than he had been the night before. He said he would stop at the next town before we got there but never did. Just before reaching a town he would say to Shorty, drive fast but don't get pinched. I vomited in the car all over the back seat and grips.

Stephenson didn't try to comfort her in anyway, telling her he thought she was dying. At one time during the ride, he said to Gentry, "This takes guts to do this, Gentry. She is dying."

Madge also heard him say that he had been in a worse mess than this before and got out of it. As Shorty drove, Stephenson and Gentry drank during the entire trip. Madge was able to hear some of what they were talking about. She would later say that Stephenson said that he had power and had made $250,000. He bragged that his word was law.

They drove straight to his house and pulled into the garage. Someone was at the front door and Stephenson told Shorty to go see who it was. Shorty came back and said it was Mrs. Oberholtzer, Madge's mother. Then Stephenson said, "You will stay right here until you marry me."

Stephenson, who was thirty-three but looks much older in his photos, told her to say her injuries were because of an auto accident and repeated several times, in order to make her compliant and fearful, that he was the law and the power.

One of the men carried her up the stairs to the loft above the garage. Again, the Grand Dragon did nothing to help her pain, leaving her alone all night. The next day, Klinck came and woke her up saying she had to go home. Madge asked where Stephenson was and Klinck said he didn't know. She begged Klinck, a big man, to take her home in the Cadillac but he said he'd call a cab. Finally, he relented. Dressing her, her carried her downstairs and placed her in the back seat of Stephenson's car and drove to her house. Madge finished her statement:

> I said to him to drive up in the driveway. He did and then carried me into the house and upstairs and into my bed. It was about noon Tuesday when we got into the house.
>
> I, Madge Oberholtzer, am in full possession of all my mental faculties and understand what I am saying. The foregoing statements have been read to me and I have made them as my statements and they are all true. I am sure that I will not recover from this illness, and I believe that death is very near to me, and I have made all of the foregoing statements as my dying declaration and they are true.

The Oberholtzers lived in Irvington Park, a pretty neighborhood in Indianapolis near the prestigious Butler University where the family attended the Tudor-style Irvington United Methodist Church. Madge's father worked as a postal clerk. She had studied English, mathematics, zoology, and logic at Butler but dropped out at the end of her junior year. Described by a friend as "an independent soul, yet timid. I don't think anybody disliked Madge, but she didn't make a great effort to make people like her, either," Madge was working as the manager of the Indiana Young People's Reading Circle, a special section of the Indiana Department of Public Instruction when she met Stephenson. She also did some work for him and saw him socially as well.

Panicked when her daughter hadn't yet returned, Matilda Oberholtzer called attorney Ada J. Smith. The Oberholtzers were meeting with him two days later at his office when Eunice Schultz, a boarder at their home, heard groaning sounds and saw a large man carrying Madge up their stairs. "She'd been in car accident," he told Schultz who immediately called Dr. Kingsbury.

"She was in a state of shock; her body was cold," said Kingsbury, who hurried to the house. Oberholtzer told the doctor that she both knew she was going to die and wanted to die but wouldn't say more. He pressed her and soon learned what had happened.

HOLD SEX-KLANSMAN ON ASSAULT CHARGE

*Indianapolis Grand Jury Accuses D. C. Stephenson
of Attacking Young Woman*

ALSO INDICTS TWO OTHERS

*Former Klan Leader Has Been Prominent
in Indiana Republican Circles*

New York Times, Thursday, April 3, 1924

D. C. Stephenson, former Grand Dragon of the Ku Klux Klan in Indiana was indicted today by the Marion County Grand Jury on five charges in connection with an alleged attack on Miss Madge Oberholtzer of Indianapolis.

Indictments also were returned against Earl Klinck and Earl Gentry said to have been companions of Stephenson.

Stephenson who was arrested last night on affidavits filed by George E. Oberholtzer, father of the girl, gained prominence as organized of the Klan in twenty-one Northern states.

The indictments charge Stephenson with assault and battery with intent to kill, assault and battery with intent to rape, malicious mayhem, kidnapping and conspiracy to kidnap. . . .

Judge James A. Collins fixed Stephenson's bond at $25,000 which was provided. . . .

Mr. Oberholtzer caused affidavits to be filed, he said, on statements Miss Oberholtzer made regarding a train ride to Hammond, Ind., on March 15 and return trip by automobile. Mr. Oberholtzer said the girl was taken forcibly to Hammond after having been made to drink liquor at Stephenson's home here.

Other than to say the action was a "political move," Stephenson would not make a statement.

Miss Oberholtzer, who is 28 years old, was unconscious tonight. A blood transfusion was made but the results will not be known for from twenty-four to forty-eight hours, according to Dr. John Kingsbury, her physician. Dr. Kingsbury held out little hope for the girl who took poison after the alleged attack. . . .

Stephenson, who is reputed to be well off, was until recently President of the Central States Coal Company and since coming to Indianapolis from the southern part of the state has concerned himself considerably with Indiana politics.

During the Gubernatorial campaign of 1924 Stephenson is said to have been active on behalf of Governor Ed Jackson and to have been elected with the support of the Klan. Soon after the campaign Stephenson, according to Harry M. Smith of Elkhart, Secretary of the Elkhart Klavern, was read out of the organization. Mr. Smith, who volunteered his statement after learning that Stephenson had been indicted here, said that Stephenson was "banished with complete ostracism" and that "all Klansmen now are barred from speaking to him or communicating with him in any way will result in their being banished."

Stephenson's attorneys fought to keep Madge's death-bed statement out of the courtroom but were overruled.

ADMITS DYING STATEMENT

*Court Will Hear Girl's Charges against Stephenson,
Ex-Klansman*

---

*The Dying Declaration of Madge Oberholtzer,
after Some Deletions, Will Be Admitted in Evidence Tomorrow
in the Trial of D. C. Stephenson, Earl Gentry and Earl Klinck,
Charged with Murdering the Woman*

New York Times, **Friday, October 30, 1925**

Violence, drunkenness, and rage were part of Stephenson's operating style. Married and divorced numerous times, he abandoned one wife when she was pregnant and had battered a few women, threatening to kill one if she didn't have sex with him. His dominant personality, ruthlessness, and conniving character helped him rise through the ranks of the KKK and become supremely powerful.

D. C. knew how to rile up crowds with his hate-filled messages. He rallied against blacks, Jews, and Catholics as well as the Eastern Europeans who had come to America to work in the mills and manufacturing plants in Northwest Indiana. While major industrial cities and the newspapers that served them such as the *Gary Post Tribune* and the *Hammond Times* were willing to stand up to the Klan even though they received numerous death threats, the rural areas flocked to Stephenson's rallies, growing at times to twenty thousand people strong. According to Trent D. Pendley, author of *Indiana Jewish History: The Jewish History of the Indiana Dunes Country, 1830–1950,* almost half-a-million Hoosiers belonged to the Ku Klux Klan during the 1920s. Right-wing women founded the WKKK and, like their male counterparts, demanded the supremacy of white, native-born Protestants. They opposed immigration, racial equality, Jewish-owned businesses, and parochial schools. The WKKK looked to their white-hooded men to protect them and their families from moral decay.

Though Stephenson controlled most of the state legislatures who had come to him to get elected as well as the governor, Marion

The Ku Klux Klan at a funeral in Gary, Indiana. At the height of their power, the KKK ran Indiana's government. Photo courtesy of the Indiana University Northwest Calumet Archives.

County prosecutor William Henderson Remy, a graduate of Indiana University's law school who was sometimes known, because of his youth and his looks, as the "boy prosecutor," wasn't one of them.

The trial was a political bloodbath for the Klan-connected politicians as more and more details came out. Stephenson, the former kingmaker, was abandoned by those he'd helped get elected and he turned against them.

EX-DRAGON OF KLAN WILL GET LIFE TERM:
D. C. STEPHENSON CONVICTED FOR DEATH
OF ABDUCTED GIRL

Manitowoc Herald-Times, **Monday, November 16, 1925**

Though his defense attorneys worked hard to convince the jury that Stephenson had been set up by political rivals, and well, maybe,

Oberholtzer wasn't that nice of a girl anyway and probably deserved what had happened to her, the jury returned a guilty verdict.

CALL MAYOR TOOL OF INDIANA KLAN

Investigators Give Out Contract, Alleging Duvall of Indianapolis Signed It

PAPER PLEDGED PLACES

Agreed to Appoint Only Men Endorsed by Stephenson, Then Grand Dragon

New York Times, Thursday, October 7, 1926

Thomas H. Adams, head of the State Republican Editorial Association committee which has been investigating alleged Klan corruption in State politics and government, made public today the first instalment of a mass of alleged evidence by which he seeks to expose and drive from public office the political ring he charges has overthrown constitutional government in Indiana.

INDIANA ASSEMBLY LINKED TO "DRAGON"

Murder Trial Witnesses Tell How Legislators Consulted Accused Klan Chief

PRIMARY TACTICS REVEALED

An Insight into D. C. Stephenson's Activities during the Last Primary Campaign and at the 1925 Session of the Indiana Legislature Was Given Here Today at the Murder Trial of the Former Ku Klux Klan Leader

New York Times, Tuesday, November 10, 1925

Thomas H. Adams, head of a committee investigating Klan corruption in State politics and government, made public the first installment of evidence by which he seeks to expose and drive from office the political ring he charges have overthrown the constitutional government in Indiana.

It was in the form of photographic copy of an alleged contract signed by D. C. Stephenson, former Grand Drago on the Ku Klux Klan and now serving a life sentence for the murder of Madge Oberholtzer, by Mayor J. Duvall of Indianapolis, dated February 12, 1925.

"In return for the political support of D. C. Stephenson in the event I am elected Mayor of Indianapolis, Ind. I promise not to appoint any person or member of the Board of Public Works without they first have the endorsement of D. C. Stephenson," the document reads. "I also agree and promise to appoint Claude Worley as Chief of Police and Earl Klenic as captain.

Signed by me this 12th day of February, 1925.

After Stephenson's conviction, Remy had the former Grand Dragon testify regarding the large sums of money he'd contributed to Jackson when he was running for the governorship in 1924. It was money that Jackson had somehow forgotten to report and denied receiving. Stephenson produced a canceled check for $2,500 made out to Jackson in support of his claim. Jackson, in turn, said that the $2,500 was for a horse he'd bought from D. C. but, unfortunately, the horse had died while eating a corncob. Contemporary thought was that Jackson was a horse's ass if he thought anyone would believe that.

The Marion County Grand Jury indicted Jackson on charges of bribery and the *Indianapolis Star* wrote "Indiana bows its head in shame."

CRISIS DRAWS NEAR IN INDIANA SCANDAL

*Public Opinion Now Demands Full Light
on Corruption Confessed by Stephenson*

PROSECUTOR GATHERS DATA

*Remy's Apparent Determination to Act Causes
Trembling among Many Higher Ups*

GOVERNOR SCORNS CONVICT

*But There Is Wide Belief That Jackson Will Yet Pardon
the Former Klan Leader*

New York Times, Sunday, July 17, 1927

Amid the political upheaval in Indiana and Indianapolis, brought about by the sending of D. C. Stephenson, former Grand Dragon of the Ku Klux Klan in this State, to prison for life on a murder conviction, one question is constantly asked by the general public: Will Governor Jackson, before he retires from office, pardon Stephenson?

Unfortunately, though Jackson was obviously guilty, he was acquitted on a technicality and actually got to finish out his term. But the upside? He didn't feel inclined to pardon Stephenson after that.

The trial helped destroy the Klan's influence not only in Indiana— three years later Klan membership in Indiana had dropped to around ten thousand—but also throughout the country.

Though Stephenson went to prison, always wily and working the angles, an investigating committee heard that there was a move to have Stephenson declared insane. That didn't work, but he ultimately was paroled in 1950 with the stipulation he live and work in Illinois. Instead he moved to Minnesota. Arrested, he spent six more years in prison and then was released by Indiana governor George Craig. His next stop was Seymour, Indiana, where he married for a third time, but that didn't last after he was arrested for trying to force a sixteen-year-old girl into his car. Paying a fine of $300 in cash, Stephenson next traveled to Tennessee where he married a Sunday school teacher, conveniently forgetting to tell her about his past. Of course, he was still married to his third wife, but those were mere details in a life of violating the law. He worked for the *Jonesboro Herald and Tribune,* writing copy and maintaining the presses, and also invented a type-cleaning machine that he sold to other newspapers.

On June 28, 1966, he was carrying a basket of fruit he'd bought for his wife into the house when he collapsed and died in her arms. She knew nothing about his past and wouldn't learn about it until twelve years later when a reporter told her the story of the Grand Dragon.

The Indiana Hotel was torn down in the 1990s says Brian Poland, director of Historic Preservation for the City of Hammond. As for Oberholtzer's death, Poland says, "I don't want to minimalize what she went through, it was horrible, but her sacrifice led to the downfall of the Ku Klux Klan in Indiana and, really, in the U.S. She really was a hero."

11

Double Indemnity

TELLS JURY OF DECKER'S HASTE TO BURY BODY

*Bourbon Undertaker Testifies Fred Bough Cheap Casket
and Wanted Funeral Held Next Day*

DESCRIBES BROTHER'S ACTS

*Witnesses Tell of Identification of Lovett's Body
by Cal and Fred*

Indianapolis Star, **Wednesday, June 8, 1921**

Identification of the body of Leroy Lovett by Fred and Cal Decker as that of their brother, Virgil Decker, and how on Sunday, a few hours after death occurred, Fred purchased a cheap casket, engaged a minister, arranged for the digging of the grave and announced that the funeral would be held at 2 o'clock on the following day, was told about today by witnesses who testified at the trial of Virgil Decker, charged with Lovett's murder. Homer Dilly, Bourbon undertaker, told of Fred Decker's apparent haste as he was arranging for the funeral and told his reference to the insurance Virgil carried.

"Fred Decker never came very near the body," continued Dilly. "He said it looked like Virgil and the clothes were Virgil's." "I then asked Cal about it," Dilly continued, "and he said don't you think I know my brother, hell, I know him by the tattoo on his arm. Virgil and I had our arms tattooed at the same time in Fort Wayne."

"I then called Cal's attention to the fact that the mark on his arm was old while that on the body's arm was a fresh one. Cal made no answer."

Three Months Earlier

Tenderly touching the hair of the young man who lay on the undertaker's table, Lydia Decker broke into sobs as she told Dr. Novitas B. Aspinall, the coroner of Marshall County, the body was indeed that of her son, Virgil Decker. In agreement were Virgil's brothers, Fred and Cal. To further help make the identification, a letter found in the coat worn by the deceased was addressed to Virgil and was from his brother Fred.

In a hurry to bury her son as quickly as possible, Mrs. Decker ordered the casket but managed to find time to ask when she might expect the check from the insurance company.

Unfortunately for the Deckers, they didn't get Virgil in the ground fast enough. The parents of Leroy Lovett, Virgil's good friend who was similar to him in looks, also identified the body. Not as Virgil but of Leroy.

"The minute I pulled back the sheet I knew it was my boy," said Sam Lovett, while his wife Hattie noted several identifying characteristics including a birthmark and tattoo.

DEATH IN THE NIGHT

Warsaw Times Union, **February 24 and 25, 1951**

On the night of March 12, 1921—almost 30 years ago—the engineer of a fast Pennsylvania freight train stiffened as he approached Robinson's crossing, a short distance west of Atwood. The glare of his headlight revealed a buggy, with no horse harnessed to it, standing directly in the path of the locomotive. He applied his brakes, but it was too late to avoid striking the buggy, which was reduced to kindling wood. The crew jumped from the train, and soon found the body of a youth lying between the two tracks. He was alive, but unconscious. The injured young man was placed aboard a westbound passenger train and taken to Bourbon. There he died a few hours later without having spoken a word.

Almost immediately following the accident, Sheriff Charles Moon and Dr. Aspinall had questions. Where was the horse and why wasn't it with the carriage on the train tracks? That one was easily answered. Hoofprints led to the Decker farm not far away and a look at the harness showed it had been sliced through. The horse had done what horses always do, headed home to the barn.

It was also quickly determined that the dead man had been tortured. His jaw was broken, and Excelsior—a type of wood fiber—had been jammed into 'his mouth preventing his screams from being heard. Marks on his neck indicated someone had attempted to strangle him.

This was no buggy accident. This was murder.

Still not knowing the identity of the corpse (both the Deckers and the Lovetts were insistent that the body was that of their son), Sheriff Moon went searching for either Virgil or Leroy, dead or alive. At a summer cottage along the Tippecanoe River, about a mile from the railroad crossing where the faked accident had been staged, Moon found more than enough evidence to show a grisly crime had been committed. The cottage was owned by C. A. Rovenstein, a merchant at Atwood and owner of the farm on which Fred Decker lived. The place was quickly given a name by the reporters who were covering the case.

THE MURDER COTTAGE

Fort Wayne Journal Gazette, **Tuesday, March 15, 1921**

The interior of the riverside three-room cottage showed unmistakable evidence of a fierce battle having taken place there. Investigators found blood stains on the walls and doors. A blood spot on a table showed under a microscope that it contained human hair. There were also blood spots on the outside of the door. Footprints in the sand led from the door to the river. The footprints showed that the person had one shoe on and one shoe off. That matched the body found on the railroad tracks, which also had a shoe only on one foot. A bloodstained coat found in the shack was identified as that worn by Lovett, when he left home last Friday night.

The Deckers continued to insist the body was that of Virgil. And well they should have. Authorities learned Virgil, who worked on the farm for his brother, made $40 a month plus board, yet three months before the murder he'd taken out three insurance policies on himself totaling $24,000 at a cost of $500 a year in premiums. Two of them paid double indemnity in case of accidental death. You don't have to be good at math to figure out Virgil couldn't afford the premiums.

As for the dueling sets of parents, Aspinall was able to put a quick end to that. Asking Lydia Decker the color of her son's eyes and receiving blue for an answer, he pulled open one of the eyelids. Brown, the color of Leroy Lovett's eyes.

"DOUBLE" OF DECKER SLAIN, SAYS CORONER

Indianapolis Star, **Tuesday, March 15, 1921**

Believing the killing of Leroy Lovett, 19 years old of Elkhart, Ind., the result of a plot between Fred Decker and his brother Virgil of Kosciusko county to collect $24,000 insurance, Coroner Novitas B. Aspinall of Marshall county, tonight made a statement in which he unfolded his convictions as to the motives for the alleged murder of the youth who was found in a dying condition along the Pennsylvania railroad tracks at a crossing near Atwood Saturday night.

In expressing his convictions, Coroner Aspinall noted the marked resemblance between Virgil and Leroy and how Fred Decker was the beneficiary of a large policy on Virgil's life.

At the joint inquest held at Bourbon, both Aspinall and Coroner Charles A. Kelly of Kosciusko County stated their belief that Lovett had been hit over the head with a piece of iron, most likely a buggy tire.

> The body is then believed to have been taken to the river but later was brought back into the cottage and then taken to the railroad track where it was placed on the tracks and a buggy owned by Virgil Decker placed on the track also the coroner believes to make it appear a train had struck the buggy and killed the youth. Coroner Aspinall said he did not believe the body had been in the buggy when the vehicle was placed on the track and as evidence cited that the body was not mangled. The body was found fifty feet away from the spot where the buggy was struck.

Warrants were issued for the arrest of Virgil Decker as well as his brothers and mother. Virgil made up a series of stories for what had happened at the cottage. In one, he and Leroy were cooking chickens at the cottage when a man named Guy killed his friend.

The Deckers pled not guilty.

The trial began on June 1, 1921, with Prosecutor H. W. Graham, assisted by L. R. Stookey attempting to prove that there was a family conspiracy in the murder of Lovett.

A BRILLIANT DEFENSE

Warsaw Times Union, **February 24 and 25, 1951**

> The defense attorneys presented a strong case. They contended that there was no conspiracy to defraud the insurance compa-

nies. Fred Decker's father-in-law, a man of wealth, testified that he had assisted Fred in meeting payments on his farm, and that Fred had no desperate need for money. It was claimed that Virgil, in taking out the insurance, had the idea that he could make himself rich in 20 years for less than $500 a year. The defense proved that all the insurance agents had first solicited Virgil—that he did not first seek them. It was pointed out that if Virgil had wanted to disappear, he would not have gone to Marion where he was well known. Virgil's reputation in the community had been good. His confession that Guy had been the slayer was accepted by the defense. Two witnesses testified to having seen a stranger near the cottage and the farm home on the night of the crime. Virgil was in Atwood several times during the day, and it was claimed that he would not have left Leroy in the cottage alone—to wander out, be seen, and spread an alarm.

DECKER DRAWS LIFE PENALTY

Murdered Pal Jury Decides on First Vote—Five Additional Ballots Said to Have Been Taken to Determine Punishment

---

Boy Shows No Emotion

Calmly Hears Reading of Verdict without Comment— Sings While Waiting

Indianapolis Star, Saturday, June 11, 1921

Virgil Decker, 19 years old of Elkhart, Ind., was found guilty of first degree murder by a jury in the Kosciusko Circuit court to-night. He was convicted of the murder of Leroy Lovett, 20 years old, his chum and "double." The jury fixed the punishment at life imprisonment.

The verdict was returned at 6:45 o'clock this evening three hours and thirty-five minutes after the case had been given to the jury. Six ballots were taken, it is understood. He was convicted on the first ballot according to reports and the other ballots were taken to fix the punishment. Some favored the electric chair, it is said.

DEATH PENALTY ASKED

The State Had Asked for the Death Penalty during Its Closing Arguments

R. Stookey made the closing argument for the state. With the blood stained door from the "murder cabin," the blood-soaked pillows, a blood stained couch top and the death weapon—a heavy piece of iron with which Virgil confessed to having struck Lovett over the head arranged in a heap before the jury. Attorney Stookey made an eloquent plea before the jurying asking for conviction. Each blood stained article was shown to the jury and pointing to the blood stained articles, Mr. Stookey, in closing said: "The blood of Leroy Lovett and vengeance. Gentlemen of the jury these mute evidences cry out for vengeance Gentlemen of the jury, if you have any sympathy and grief the place for that is at the grave of Leroy Lovett."

The charges against Lydia Decker and her two sons were eventually dismissed for lack of sufficient evidence.

SELECTED BIBLIOGRAPHY

Abbott, Karen. "Murder Wasn't Very Pretty": The Rise and Fall of D. C. Stephenson." *Smithsonian.com.* August 30, 2012. http://www.smithsonianmag.com/history/murder-wasnt-very-pretty-the-rise-and-fall-of-dc-stephenson-18935042/#76dOO67B4yeEorFT.99.

Boysun, Mara. "Black Widow Murdered Dozens at Farm." *New York Daily News,* November 30, 2014.

Crumrin, Tim. "Sex (in Context)." *wthhistory: The Rise and Decline of a Small Town.* June 18, 2014. https://wthhistory.wordpress.com/2014/06/.

The Encyclopedia of Cleveland History. "Cleveland Water Cure Establishment." Last modified June 25, 1997. http://ech.case.edu/cgi/article.pl?id=CWCE.

History of Warrick, Spencer, and Perry Counties, Indiana: from the earliest time to the present; together with interesting biographical sketches, reminiscences, notes, etc. Perry County, IN: Goodspeed, 1885.

Journal of the Bizarre. "The Strange Disappearance of Luella Mabbitt." 2015. http://www.journalofthebizarre.com/2015/07/the-strange-disappearance-of-luella.html.

Liebowitz, Irving. "The Dying Declaration of Madge Oberholtzer: The Key Evidence in the 1925 Trial of D. C. Stephenson." In *My Indiana.* Englewood Cliffs, NJ: Prentice-Hall, 1964.

MacGregor, Robert. "Rat Poison Advertising in America: The First 100 Years." *St. John Fisher College.* 2012. http://fisherpub.sjfc.edu/cgi/viewcontent.cgi?article=1084&context=nepca.

Pendley, Trent D. *Indiana Jewish History: The Jewish History of the Indiana Dunes Country, 1830–1950.* Indianapolis: Indiana Jewish Historical Society Publications, 2004.

Stoner, Andrew. *Notorious 92: Indiana's Most Heinous Murders in All 92 Counties.* Fresno, CA: Rooftop Publishing, 2007.

Tucker, Todd. *Notre Dame vs. the Klan: How the Fighting Irish Defeated the Ku Klux Klan.* Chicago: Loyola Press, 2004.

Van Beck, Todd. "The Harrison Horror, Grave Robbing and the Invention of the Burial Vault 1878." *The Indiana Funeral Directors Association.* http://www .infda.org/.

Wilheim, Robert. *Murder by Gaslight.* 2012. http://www.murderbygaslight.com/.

Wimmer, Curt P. A. *History of the College of Pharmacy of the City of New York Included in Columbia University.* N.p.: Google eBook, 1929.

NEWSPAPERS AND OTHER SOURCES

Ancestry.com

Bremen Enquirer (IN)

Cannelton Reporter (IN)

Chicago Daily Tribune

Chicago Tribune

Cincinnati Enquirer

Courier-Journal (Louisville, KY)

Crawfordsville Weekly Journal

Daily Evening Bulletin (Maysville, KY)

The Daily Review

Daily Times (News Brunswick, NJ)

Daily Tobacco Leaf-Chronicle (Clarksville, TN)

Democrat and Chronicle (Rochester, NY)

East Chicago Washington Anvil, 1925

Evansville Courier

Evansville Journal

Evansville Press

Evening Bulletin (Maysville, KY)

Evening Star (Washington, DC)

Familysearch.com

Fiery Cross

Gary Post Tribune

Goshen Democrat

Greencastle Star Press (IN)

Hammond Times (also titled *Indiana Harbor Times and Lake County Times*)

Historic Indianapolis.com

Indiana State Supreme Court Trial Transcripts

Indianapolis Journal

Indianapolis News

Indianapolis Star

Indianapolis State Sentinel

Jasper Weekly Courier
Lake County Times
Logansport Pharos-Tribune
Louisville Ledger
Manitowoc Herald-Times
Marshall County Republican (IN)
Nashville Union and American
New York Times
News-Herald (Hillsboro, OH)
Oshkosh Daily Northwestern (WI)
Phillipsburg Herald (KS)
Plymouth Democrat
Plymouth Republican
Rockport Democrat (IN)
San Francisco Call
San Francisco Chronicle
South Bend News-Times
South Bend Tribune
Sterling Standard (IL)
St. Louis Post Dispatch
St. Paul's Daily Globe (MN)
http://unknownmisandry.blogspot.com/2014/03/annie-wagner-sympathetic
    -indiana-serial.htm
Vidette Messenger (Valparaiso, IN)
Warsaw Indianian
Warsaw Times Union
Waterloo Daily Courier (IA)
Weekly Republican (Plymouth)
Wilkes-Barre Times (PA)

JANE SIMON AMMESON is a freelance writer and photographer who specializes in travel, food, and personalities. She writes frequently for the *Times of Northwest Indiana, Chicago Life Magazine, Edible Michiana, AAA Home & Away, Experience Curacao, Cleveland Magazine, Heartland Boating,* and *Lakeland Boating.* She is author of *Hauntings of the Underground Railroad: Ghosts of the Midwest, A Jazz Age Murder in Northwest Indiana,* and *East Chicago.*